TERRY J. GANDER

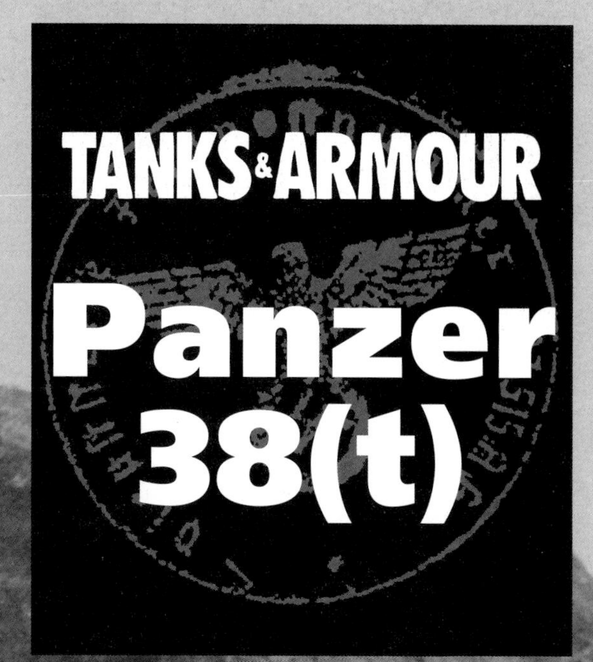

TERRY J. GANDER

Acknowledgements
This book could not have been produced without the invaluable assistance of the following people: David Fletcher, Historian at the Tank Museum (TM), Bovington, Dorset, England, and the Librarian Janice Tate; the museum's photographer, Roland Groom for original images and prints from archive material. My gratitude to Thomas Anderson *(TAn)* for access to his wonderful collection of World War Two images. Thanks to Vladimir Francev *(VF)* for supplying images from the original factory. Finally to Mark Franklin for his excellent colour artworks.

John Prigent
August 2005

Series Created by Jasper Spencer-Smith.
Design: Nigel Pell.
Military Editor: John Prigent.
Produced by JSS Publishing Limited, PO. Box 6031, Bournemouth, Dorset, BH1 9AT, England.

TITLE SPREAD: Hungarian crewmen with the PzKpfw 38(t) Ausf G on the Russian Front. *(T&A)*

ABOVE: On the way to the front, a *Panzerjäger 38(t) fur 7.62cm PaK 36(r)* is loaded on a train for delivery to a combat unit. *(T&A)*

COVER: See page 43.

First published 2006

ISBN (10) 0 7110 3091 X
ISBN (13) 978 0 7110 3091 6

Published by Ian Allan Publishing

an imprint of Ian Allan Publishing Ltd, Hersham, Surrey KT12 4RG
Printed in England by Ian Allan Printing Ltd, Hersham, Surrey KT12 4RG

0602/B3

Visit the Ian Allan Publishing website at www.ianallanpublishing.com

Contents

Chapter 1
Development

The Czech light tank soon achieved export success, not least by being taken into German service as the PzKpfw 38(t). The vehicle was so robust that it remained in service with some armies until long after World War Two.

For many observers the origins of the Czech light tank that became the German *Panzer-Kampfwagen* (PzKpfw) 38(t) might seem somewhat obscure. Not so obscure is the fact that the basic hull, chassis and running gear of the PzKpfw 38(t) proved to be so reliable, sturdy and versatile that it remained close to the core of the German armoured warfare operational scene from 1939 until 1945. Apart from the base light tank, the design proved adaptable to many other combat roles, many far from the expectations of the original designers.

Origins

Although the Czech and Slovak peoples had deep roots in history they had for generations been absorbed by the Austro-Hungarian Empire. Their independence was achieved on 15 October 1918 and acknowledged in 1919 by the Treaty of Versailles. The separate Czech and Slovak states had united to form the first Czechoslovak Republic but unfortunately the boundaries were disputed by many of the neighbouring states created by the Versailles Treaty and contained dissenting minorities, particularly of German and Hungarian descent. These, compounded by political differences between the Czechs and Slovaks, created internal security problems to add to the boundary disputes. The new Republic was therefore forced to direct a large proportion of national resources to defence.

Fortunately the Republic had major assets at its disposal, the Czech lands having been the main industrial centre of the old Austro-Hungarian Empire. The western sector, including Prague, Milovice and Pilsen, held the main centres of the Empire defence industry and was ready, able and willing to provide the needs of the new Republic. The skilled engineers, designers and workers here were among the best in Europe, and their worth was demonstrated by armament exports to many other nations as well as by sales at home.

Within this defence industrial infrastructure, two concerns dominated. They were Škoda and ČKD. Both were large established

ABOVE: The right-hand side of a Pz 38(t) *neue Art* reconnaissance tank shows the most obvious differences from the original tank: a new turret with an improved gun in a modified mounting. Also visible is the redesigned exhaust pipe and silencer arrangement necessitated by the fitting of a more powerful engine. *(VF)*

conglomerates capable of designing and manufacturing all manner of weaponry from heavy ordnance to armoured cars and electrical equipment. Within such an environment the prospects of investigating tank design and production soon loomed large, most of the early work being carried out by Škoda.

Škoda was the name generally applied to the *Škodovy závodny akciová společnost*, the Škoda Enterprises Inc, based at Pilsen. Although it was primarily an ordnance concern (it supplied all the new nation's artillery in all its forms as well as having major export sales), during the 1920s it devised several advanced armoured car designs and by the 1930s was in a position to have its LT vz.35 light tank (LT – *Lehký Tank* – light tank; vz – *vgzor* – model) accepted as the light tank for the Czechoslovak Army cavalry arm. As with so many of its contemporary counterparts, the LT vz.35 was considered to have too many inherent shortcomings for comfort. As early as 1938 a replacement was under consideration and a series of trials and tests were established to decide which one to select.

Enter ČKD. ČKD stood for *Českomoravaská-Kolben-Dančk*, usually known as ČKD a.s., the a.s. denoting Incorporated or Inc. The original company was formed in 1871 as a machine manufacturer and had merged with an electrical machinery company in 1921 and a second engineering company in 1927 to become the second-largest company in Czechoslovakia. It was soon using its considerable resources to manufacture everything from machine tools to automobiles. At one point it obtained a licence to manufacture Carden-Loyd tankettes and was soon selling its own derivatives to the Czechoslovak army (and abroad). It also shared in the production of the Army's LT vz.35. Not content with home sales ČKD also sought to expand into export markets.

Although busy throughout most of the 1920s period, both the major concerns invested heavily in new plant, machinery and the development of new products. The point was soon reached where the resultant capacity became available for export sale prospects to be considered. They duly materialised.

ABOVE: A TNH-P under test in England. Although superior in many ways to British tanks of the period the TNH-P was thought too cramped for the crew, so was not ordered. This may have been just as well since the German annexation of Czechoslovakia would have prevented exports. Note that the rarely-seen central headlamp is fitted. *(VF)*

By 1931 Czechoslovakia came in at number three in terms of arms exports world wide.

As far as armoured vehicles were concerned the main ČKD product of the mid-1930s was the AH series of tankettes (tančík) and light weapon carriers. ČKD also shared in the preparation and production of the Škoda LT vz.35 to meet the demands of the Czech Army more rapidly and to fulfil export orders from nations such as Bulgaria and Romania. However, ČKD also undertook some tank development of its own even though it lost out to Škoda in the competition for the Czech Army's light tank requirement, the requirement being met by the Škoda LT vz.35.

Not to be outdone ČKD still went ahead with light tank development with a view to export sales. The result was larger and more combat effective than the tankettes of the period and was marketed under the code name of TNH. The first prototypes of the TNH appeared during late 1935, the head designer being Dipl.Ing. Alexander Surin, a Russian émigré.

Thanks to the incorporation of few frills and various well-proven engine and drive train components the TNH design soon proved to be sound with, for a light tank, an excellent combination of firepower (the TNH mounted a 37mm high-velocity gun at a time when most contemporaries were still armed with machine guns or light cannon), excellent cross-country mobility (due in no small measure to the large road wheels and spring suspension) and good protection with 25mm (0.984in) of armour at the front.

TNH export sales were not long in arriving, the first order coming from Persia (now Iran) - the order was for 50 tanks. Orders also arrived from Latvia, Peru, Romania, Sweden and Switzerland. During early 1939 the British War Mechanisation Board procured a single example for extensive testing. In the midst of all this activity and with the prospect of war with Germany looming closer and closer, the Czech Army decided that it needed a light tank more dependable than the unsatisfactory Škoda LT vz.35. It considered it had to have a better-protected vehicle with a superior cross-country capability compared to the

ABOVE: The LTH, the modified version of the TNH sold to Switzerland, had thicker armour and a modified turret cupola, a Swiss manufactured engine and guns were fitted. *(VF)*

RIGHT: A front view of the LTH shows one of those changes, the revised viewport visors in the hull and turret fronts. *(TM)*

ABOVE: A TNH tank built for Persia (now Iran). Differences to the TNH-S are very obvious: the round turret with a domed cupola, rounded position for the machine gunner, and headlamps mounted on the hull sides. *(VF)*

LEFT: An LTP tank for Peru, during obstacle crossing tests at the ČKD factory. This version used a Swedish engine specially adapted for high-altitude use. *(TM)*

ABOVE: A production-series TNH tank in the factory yard ready for shipment to Persia. It is complete with the specified light grey paint scheme and Persian markings. *(VF)*

LT vz.35 and decided to have yet another competition to determine what that vehicle might be.

Although several concerns were invited to enter proposals only two actually took part in the resultant tests. Škoda entered enhanced versions of its LT vz.35 but they displayed numerous defects and overall unreliability to the extent that they obviously needed further development before service acceptance, and by 1938 time was pressing. In contrast, ČKD entered its TNH-S (TNH-P in some sources), an improved version of the TNH ordered by Persia with a more powerful engine and an enlarged two-man turret mounting a new main gun. Not only was it trouble free but its cross-country performance proved to be excellent. There was no point in continuing the light tank selection process so it was terminated with an initial order for 150 TNH-PS suitably modified and equipped to meet Czech detail specifications established during late April 1938. The Czech Army designation became LT vz.38 and it had a crew of four.

By then the German-speaking population of the Sudetenland, where most of Czechoslovakia's fixed defences had been constructed at great expense, were making ever more strident political demands for incorporation into the Third Reich, demands that gave rise to the infamous Munich Agreement of September 1938 whereby the Sudetenland became a German province.

The new tanks were therefore needed even more urgently. Production was planned not only by ČKD but also by Škoda, Tatra and several other Czech heavy engineering concerns. ČKD was quick to prepare for series production but the Czech Army was destined to never receive its LT vz.38s. In March 1939 the German Wehrmacht marched into what was left of the Czecho-Slovak Republic after the Slovak lands decided that they would also become autonomous.

The Czech Army therefore never did receive its much-anticipated vehicles and Škoda, Tatra and the other Czech concerns never had time to establish their own production facilities. Instead the LT vz.38s about to emerge from the ČKD production line were simply taken

ABOVE: A view into the open engine bay shows the right side of the engine and the air intake manifold. The pipe running to the rear is the exhaust pipe, which also led from this side of the engine. The top of the air cleaner can just be seen over the edge of the side armour. Behind the exhaust pipe is the side of the radiator. *(TM)*

over by the *Wehrmacht* and the production facility was maintained to provide more. The LT vz.38 therefore became the *Panzer-Kampfwagen 38(t) Ausf A*. ČKD soon became the *Böhmisch-Morawische Maschinenfabrik* (BMM), while Škoda became the Škodawerke. (Not all the early TNH-S models were taken over by the Germans as a further batch of 10 were sold directly to their new Slovak Republic ally in 1941, 20 in 1942 and a final seven in 1943. The final Slovak inventory reached a total of 74, including 20 delivered from *Wehrmacht* stocks in 1943 and a further 17 in 1944.)

New Owners

Contrary to the impressions given by the German propaganda machine, in 1939 the new Panzer divisions were still woefully short of tanks. German industry was hard-pressed to meet the demands of the expanding numbers of Panzer divisions, to the extent that during 1939 some planned divisions still existed only as paper formations. The Czech LT vz.38 booty therefore came as a valuable addition to the German tank inventory and was welcomed into the ranks with gratitude. Sufficient were on hand by 1 September 1939 for a battalion with 57 of the PzKpfw 38(t) (including command tanks) to participate in the invasion of Poland. Thereafter they served on all combat fronts, apart from North Africa, until 1943 when approximately 150 were still available in depots as late as March 1945.

To get the commandeered machines into service as rapidly as possible the original Czechoslovak order of 150 vehicles was delivered to the *Wehrmacht* complete with Czech fittings and accessories, other than the fitting of Bosch electrical equipment. The Czech vz.37 models were replaced soon after the tanks were received. These vehicles became the *Panzer-Kampfwagen 38(t) Ausführung A* - (model A) 38(t). A frequent modification to the Ausf A tank was the provision of more internal working space for the radio operator/gun loader,

ABOVE: Access to the engine was good. The large hatches and relatively low height of the openings made life for mechanics a lot simpler. *(TM)*

achieved by removing two ammunition stowage bins, reducing the main 37mm tank gun ammunition capacity from 90 to 72 rounds.

As time progressed more and more German equipment installations and modifications were introduced to the production line. Two types of *Panzerbefehlswagen 38(t)* command tanks existed, the main change from the normal tanks being the addition of an extra radio in each. At company command level these command vehicles (SdKfz 266) had two rod aerials and the hull machine gun was omitted to accommodate the extra radio. At battalion and regimental levels a different radio installation was provided together with a prominent rigid frame aerial over the engine deck. These higher command level vehicles (SdKfz 267) also had the main gun was replaced by a dummy gun to provide more space for command equipment within the turret.

At least one PzKpfw 38(t) was tested with revised air filters and enhanced engine cooling measures to enable operations in hot climates. In the event the PzKpfw 38(t) was not one of the vehicles sent to North Africa but the modifications were added to the *Panzerjäger 38(t) für 7.62cm PaK 36* (SdKfz 139) issued to the *Afrika Korps*. Trials were also conducted with various flotation devices but no end result entered service.

In time the PzKpfw 38(t) light tank series reached seven *Ausführungen* in German service plus one other for export, of which more later. However, it should be stressed that following repairs and rebuilds many later developments were added to the earlier models so that differentiating between the different models becomes something of a challenge. In addition some vehicles had their Škoda 37mm guns replaced by the German Rheinmetall-Borsig 3.7cm KwK L/46.5 gun to utilise standard German ammunition supply channels – the Škoda gun fired a non-interchangeable type of ammunition.

Before the first production batch of the Ausf A had been completed preparations for a further 325 units were already in progress and this batch was manufactured with the gradual

introduction of German equipment and modifications covering the Ausf B, C and D. Combat experience revealed the need for more frontal armour and this was duly installed on the Ausf C, D, E and F. These latter two models came in a production batch of 525 light tanks. After the PzKpfw 38(t) Ausf G the base chassis were built or converted to various forms of self-propelled gun or other applications. Details of the various differences between the light tank models are outlined in the Description section. Total production of all models of light tank came to 1,396.

There was one further Czech-built TNH-based light tank model but it did not enter German service, the PzKpfw 38(t) Ausf S. During late 1939 the Swedish Army had ordered 90 TNH-Sv light tanks from ČKD but the upheavals caused by the outbreak of war meant that the production of these tanks did not commence until May 1941. By that time the German war machine had commandeered the planned 90 vehicles, the last of them being delivered during September 1941. A total of 74 of these vehicles were then handed over to what was by then known as the Slovak Free State, the old Slovakia. (What happened to the outstanding 16 vehicles has not been recorded.) Sweden was mollified by the provision of a licensing agreement to build its own TNH-Sv vehicles, the start of a process that resulted in the emergence of a separate 'Swedish' TNH family and numerous ensuing variants, all of which fall outside the scope of this account, as does mention of users other than Germany.

ABOVE: A PzKpfw 38(t) Ausf E or F, differing from earlier versions by the straight front plate for the driver and radio operator/hull gunner. There were no differences between the E and F other than the contract number under which they were built. Later models were very similar. *(T&A)*

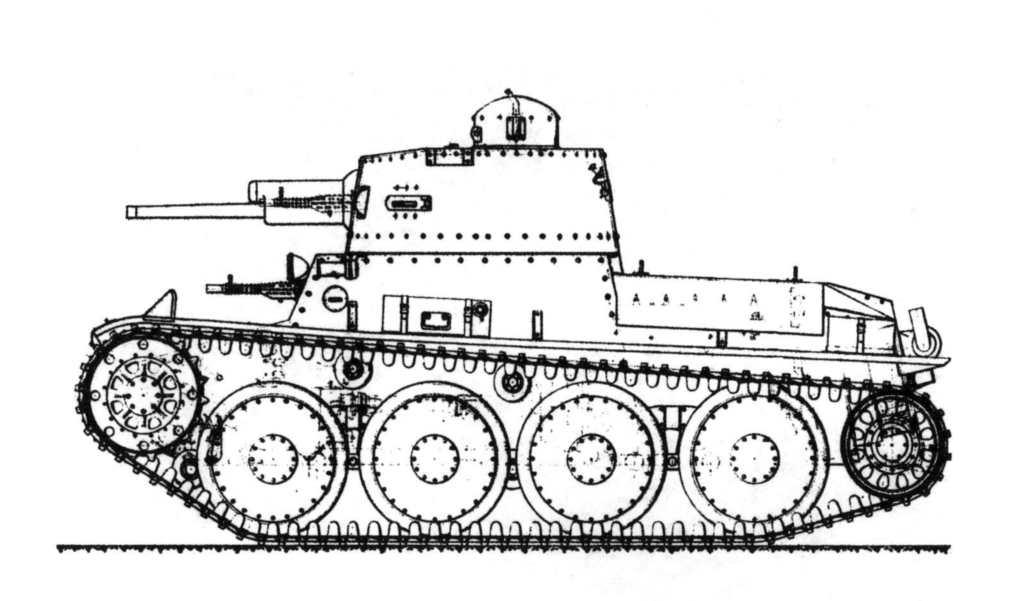

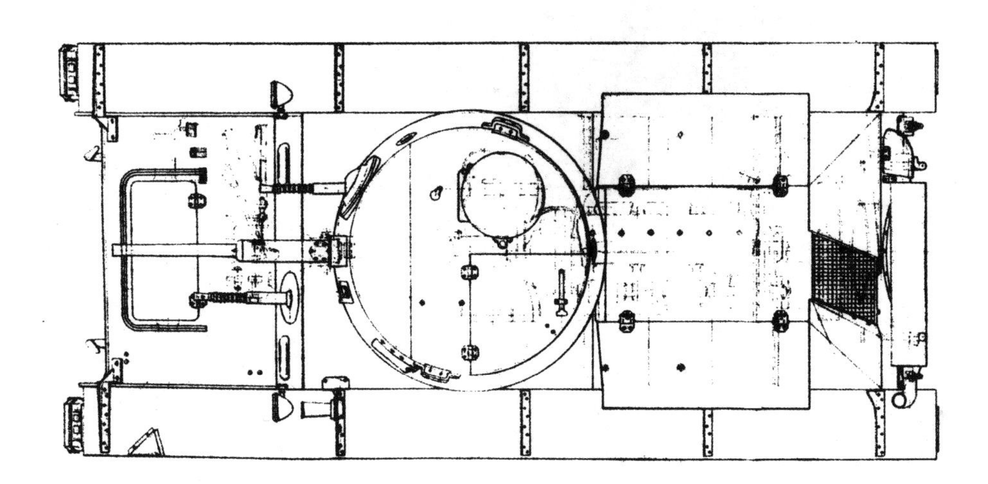

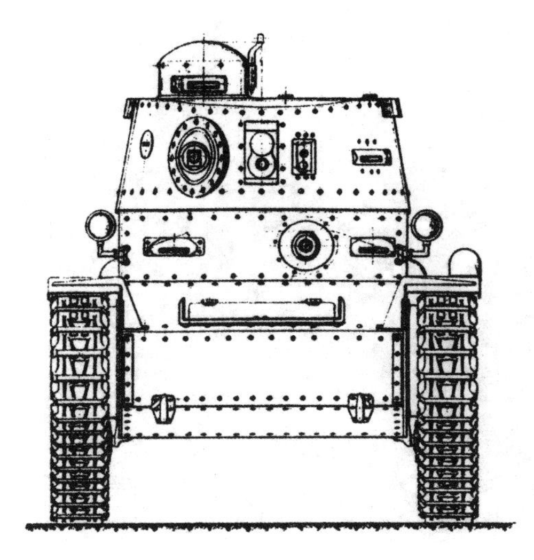

The original works three-view drawing of the TNH tank. Scale 1:35

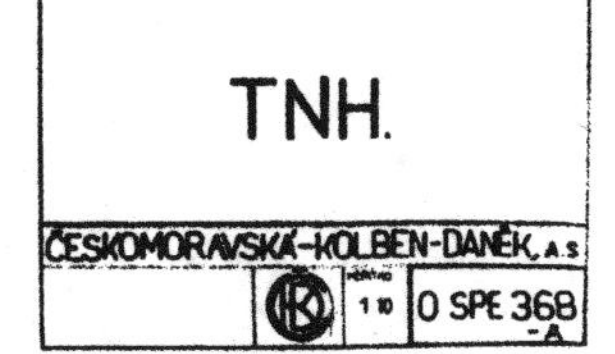

7571

LEFT: A Swiss LTH in three-colour camouflage, apparently applied with the standard Czech paints but not in the Czech-style pattern. Note the Swiss radio antenna arrangement along each side of the engine compartment, and the side-hinged covers for the engine air vent. *(TM)*

RIGHT: A Swiss LTH. Note that the turret hatches hinged backward and that the cupola did not open but was hinged with the hatch. Note also a the details of the driver's visor and of the mantlet and supressor on the 24mm Oerlikon main gun as specified by the Swiss army. *(TM)*

Chapter 2

PzKpfw 38(t) Description

The PzKpfw 38(t) was an outstanding light tank, in particular its rugged drive train and suspension were remarkable for that period.

As the PzKpfw 38(t) (t;*tchechoslowakisch*-Czech origin) series was based on the ČKD TNH-S light tank the following description is based on that vehicle. One outstanding feature of the original Czech vehicle was its reliability and ability to keep going even under the toughest conditions.

This was due in no small part to the incorporation into the drive train, and some other fundamental systems, of well proven and tested components. Following combat experience, a number of modifications and additions were inevitably introduced.

Construction

Overall, the construction of the TNH-S was simple and sound. The vehicle hull was divided by an asbestos firewall into the engine compartment and the fighting compartment, including the turret. There were two hatches in the firewall to allow access to the engine for maintenance and repairs. The hull was built-up from flat armoured plates riveted or bolted on a frame, the armour plate being produced by POLDI (*Poldina hut'* at Kladno, later known to the Germans as Poldihütte) and VHHT (*Vítovické Horní a Hutní Tezírstvo*) at Vítkovické. Frontal armour was originally 25mm (0.984in) thick and proof only against shell fragments, anti-tank rifles and light anti-tank guns, although on late production models it was increased to 50mm (1.97in). Side armour was 15mm (0.59in) thick, later increased to 30mm (1.18in) in places.

The crew of the original TNH was only three, although for the TNH-S/PzKpfw 38(t) this was increased to four as the Czechs (and the Germans) decided that the commander already had enough to do without also having to load the main gun. Two ammunition boxes were eliminated to provide the loader with the necessary working space.

The driver was seated at the right front and could also operate the centrally mounted hull machine gun once it had been locked to fire straight ahead. Next to him, on the left and in rather cramped conditions (due to the concentration of the gearbox and final drive, also radio equipment at the front of the hull)

ABOVE: A PzKpfw 38(t) Ausf A or B marked with black and white German crosses (*Balkenkreuz*) introduced after the Polish campaign. It has not yet been modified to carry the German *Notek* night driving lights. The two-digit turret number is unusual but no unit identification sign is carried. *(AN)*

was the radio operator who doubled as the hull machine gunner the gun was fully flexible in its ball mounting. The turret contained the tank commander gunner (to the left of the main gun), and the loader who also operated the co-axial machine gun. The loader's seat was to the right of commander/gunner. Observation devices were provided for all the crew and were basic but adequate. In combat, covers could be lowered over the driver's and radio operator's vision ports and bullet-proof glass vision blocks could be inserted. The commander's fixed cupola had four episcopes and a rotating periscope located just in front of the cupola. A hatch over the radio operator's position gave hull access and escape for him and the driver, while the commander and loader used the turret cupola hatch.

The fully-rotating steel turret sat in a ball-ring race with a diameter of 1.265m (49.8in). A handwheel was turned to provide manual traverse, but the turret could be traversed more quickly when necessary by disconnecting the wheel's gearing and swinging it round by hand. Elevation was controlled by a simple shoulder pad on the gun mount. As on the hull the turret's flat frontal armour was 25mm (0.984in) thick with the slightly sloping side armour being 15mm (0.59in) thick. The turret bustle at the rear was used for ready-use ammunition stowage. Armour thicknesses were increased on later models.

A rear-mounted towing hook was a standard fitting in the centre of the hull rear plate, including variants. It could be used to tow a two-wheeled fuel tank trailer or a supply trailer. Towing eyes for recovery purposes were also provided, two each at the front and rear.

Drive Train

Power for the TNH-S was provided by a six-cylinder 7,754cc Praga EPA water-cooled, in-line petrol engine delivering 130hp at 2,500rpm, sufficient for a maximum road speed of 42km/h (26mph). In some references the engine is designated as the Praga TNHPS. The name Praga shrouded the fact that the engine was actually a licence-manufactured Swedish

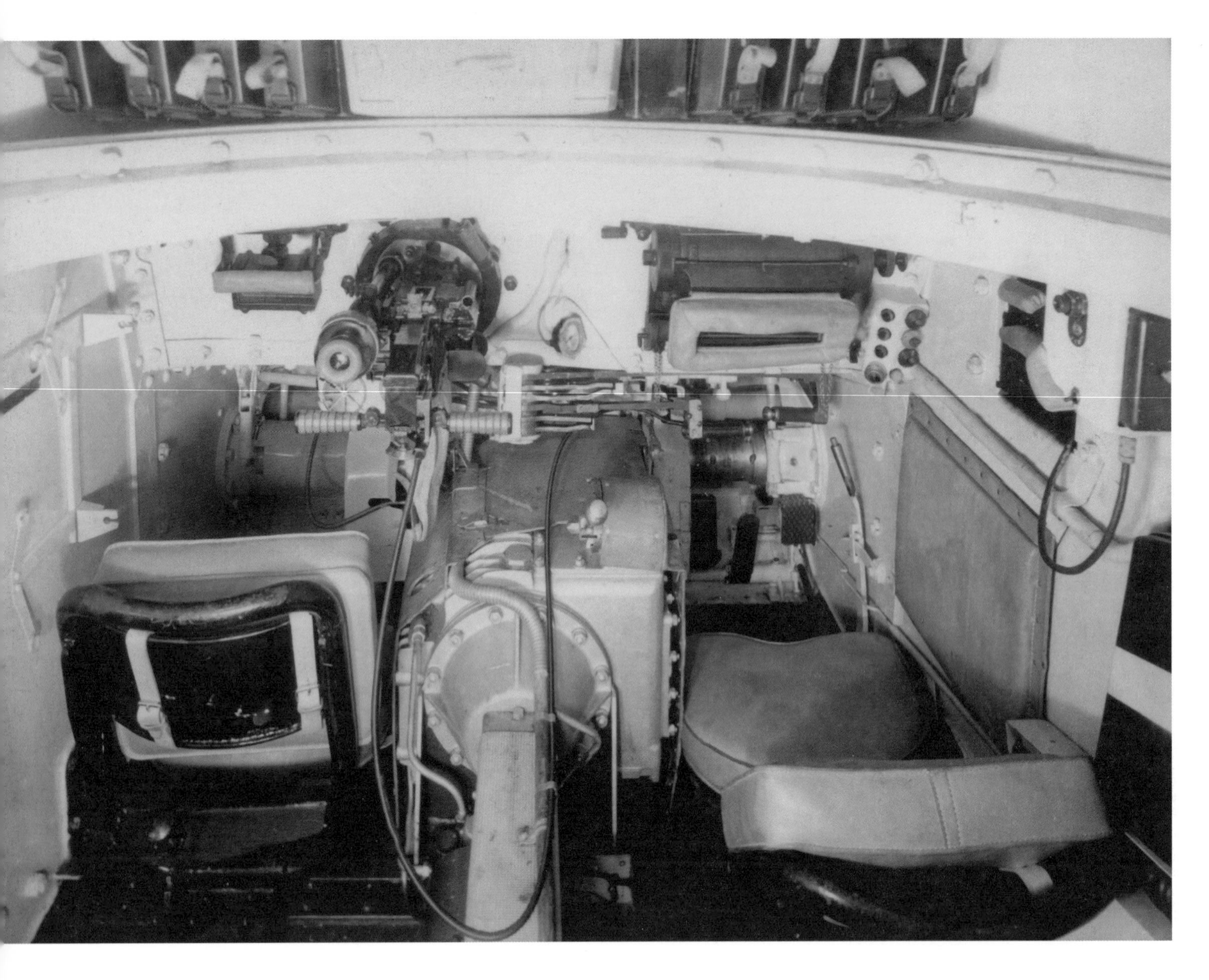

ABOVE: The front of the fighting compartment shows the driver's seat reclined to give a view of all the controls. These tanks, and their derivatives, used an unusual steering lever system, jutting sideways from the top of the gearbox instead of up from the floor. *(VF)*

Scania-Vabis 1664 truck or bus engine, apparently selected over locally developed engine sources, such as Tatra, due to its well-proven reliability and compact dimensions. Later models eventually used the Praga EPA AC on which the power output was boosted to 150hp at 2,600rpm. On the final PzKpfw 38(t) variant, the *Hetzer*, the Praga EPA AC/2 output was further improved to 160hp at 2,500rpm.

The engine ran on petrol, although alcohol-petrol mixtures could be employed. Fuel, sufficient for a cruising range of about 210km (130.5 miles), was carried in two 110-litre (24.2-gallon) tanks, one each side of the engine compartment, and pumped to the engine by either of the two available fuel pumps. A 3hp Bosch starter motor running off a 12V battery was provided although the engine could be hand-cranked via a port in the centre of a circular plate on the hull rear. Air for engine cooling was drawn in through openings in each side of the compartment, protected by the overhang of the engine deck. It was then drawn through the radiator and expelled through a grille on the rear of the engine deck, the opening size of which was adjustable (by a sliding plate, moved by hand) according to the outside air temperature. Once inside the engine compartment air was drawn through a radiator and expelled through the rear of the hull. Engine exhaust fumes were directed into a muffler located high on the rear hull plate before being expelled to the left-hand side of the vehicle. On late models this muffler was mounted at the very top of the rear plate.

Drive was taken from a large, spring-loaded dry-plate clutch and through a Cardan shaft, protected by a guard, inside the combat

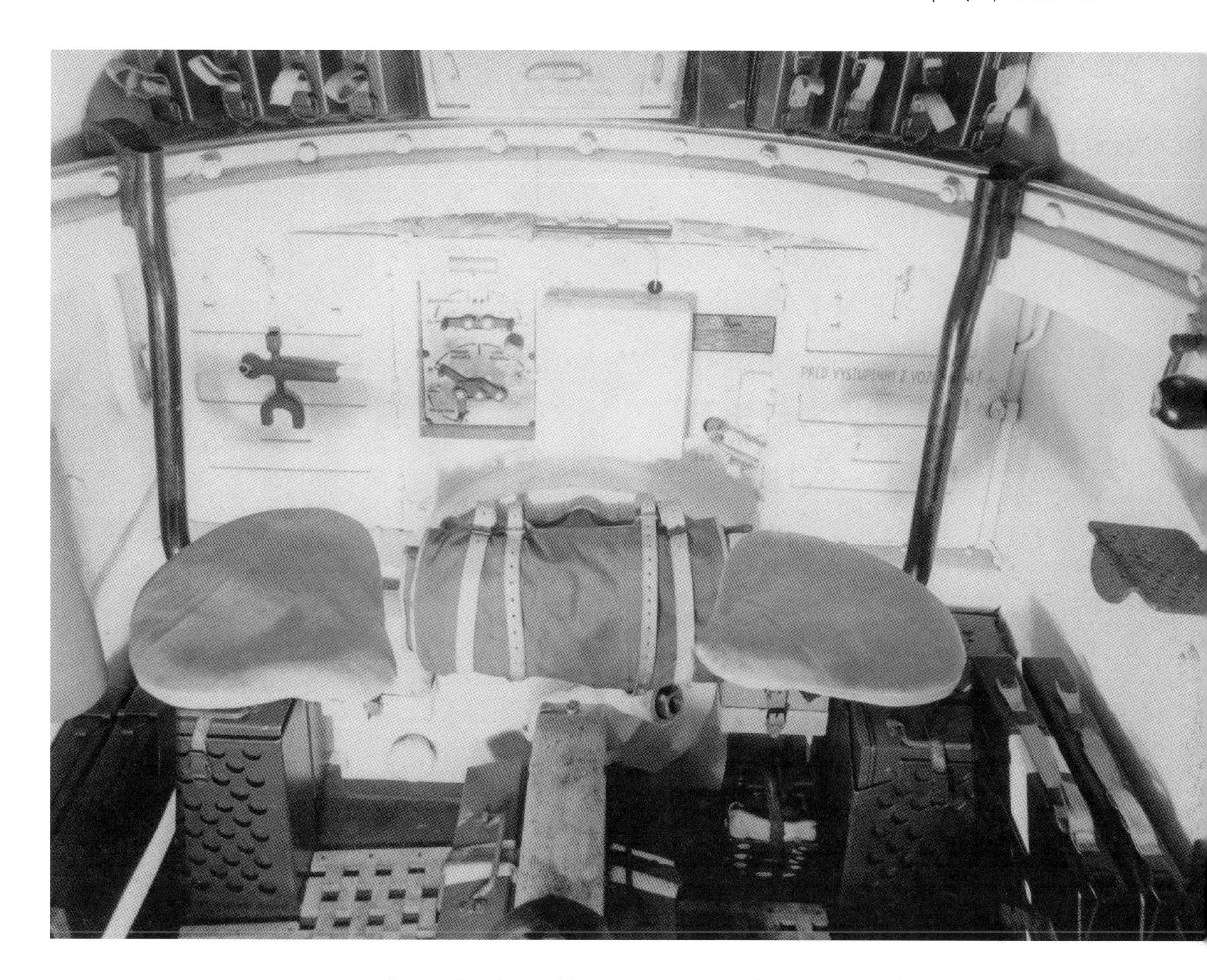

ABOVE: The rear of the fighting compartment. Note how the commander's and loader's seats were suspended from the turret ring. Above them, in the turret bustle, are stowed ammunition boxes. More ammunition was stowed under and beside each seat. *(VF)*

compartment to the gearbox located between the driver and radio operator. This gearbox was described as a Praga-Wilson EPA, concealing that it was also manufactured under licence, this time from the British company Rolls-Royce Limited. The pre-selector gearbox delivered five forward gears and one reverse, the gears being selected by the driver by using a pre-selector lever which automatically changed gear when the clutch pedal was depressed. A differential box, containing the two drive sprocket clutches and brakes, was located in front of the gearbox and connected to the drive sprockets by driving shafts.

Steering was through two horizontally mounted levers extending from the top of the steering differential to the front of the driver's position. Pulling either lever disengaged the appropriate clutch and activated the brake to turn in the selected direction. The driver could also pull a lever back and press a button on it to activate a brake on that drive shaft for a sharp turn. Pulling both levers back slowed or stopped the tank completely, and a foot pedal was provided to activate a separate parking brake. The commander and driver could communicate with each other by a three-colour signal light system using an arranged code; this was retained in German use for emergencies but rapidly supplanted by a proper interphone that could be used by all crew members.

Each of the two driving sprockets carried two 19-toothed rings, the teeth engaging slots in the track links. Each cast manganese-steel track link had two guide horns to ensure that the track remained centred by the road wheels, sprockets, idlers and return rollers and each link was 293mm (11.7in) wide and 104mm

LEFT: A PzKpfw 38(t) Ausf A in markings for the invasion of Poland. The white crosses were found to be too conspicuous, so were given black centres before the French campaign. Note the Germans, modification to the radio antenna base to carry a vertical rod antenna. The Czech-type armoured antenna that ran back along the track guard is still in place. *(T&A)*

LEFT: An Ausf G tank shows the differences to the Ausf A above. The straight front plate in front of the driver was introduced with the Ausf E, but the G can be distinguished from the E and F by the much reduced number of rivets securing the plates. *(VF)*

ABOVE: This interesting photograph shows the bolted construction of the idler wheel and reveals that the cast track links each carried different casting numbers. Note that the connecting pins do not have locking pins to stop them working loose – they could only go back toward the hull, and a plate mounted there knocked them back into place. *(AN)*

(4.095in) long. The links were connected by pins held in place by spring clips that allowed rapid changing. There were 94 track links each side and detachable spuds could be added to the extreme outer ends of the link pins to assist traction in icy or snow conditions.

Four road wheels with solid rubber tyres were fitted each side, each having a diameter of 775mm (30.5in). For added protection each running wheel was covered by an armoured disc 6mm (0.236in) thick. The wheels were mounted in pairs by short cranks with a half-elliptical leaf springing for each spring, each pair with a single central mount to the hull. The springs had 14 leaves at first, later increased to 15 as the weight of each subsequent model increased. This suspension arrangement provided a relatively smooth and comfortable ride for the crew. Two rubber-tyred track return rollers were provided on each side.

Communications

The Czech Army intended to use its then state-of-the-art vz.37 radio equipment for inter-vehicle connections. This had a telegraphic range of about 4km (2.5 miles) and employed a 3m (9ft 10in) rod aerial normally located on the front left trackguard, with the base protected by a distinctive round cylindrical-shaped cover. A second 'battle' aerial was also fitted in an armoured tube running along the left-hand side of the hull. When the German *Panzertruppen* acquired their first vehicles they installed their *FunkSprechGerät 5* (FuSprGer 5) equipment in its place to keep their inter-communication systems as compatible as possible. The FuSprGer 5 also had a maximum range of about 4km (2.5 miles) with telegraphy and 2km (1.25 miles). Power output was 10 Watts and a 2m (65.6in) rod aerial was fitted. Each tank also carried

ABOVE: Slovak army LT-38 tanks from the second batch purchased, identifiable by the serial numbers of the front two vehicles. Although purchased in 1941 all carry the white/blue/red tri-colour national shield introduced in May 1942. *(T&A)*

LEFT: A Swiss LTH, designated in service as the *Panzerwagen 39*. *(T&A)*

RIGHT: A *Panzerwagen 39* in three-colour camouflage. The Swiss added the anti-aircraft machine gun mount, almost obscurring the radio antenna on the side of the turret. *(T&A)*

RIGHT: A *Panzerwagen 39* appears to be finished in a two-colour camouflage under the prominent CH marking. Such a large marking seems likely to indicate a tank working close to the border, and to be intended to prevent Allied or German fire targeting it by mistake. *(T&A)*

signal flags and hand-held coloured lights, the latter for night operations.

The *Panzerbefehlswagen 38(t)* (SdKfz 266) command tanks held at company level had an extra radio in addition to the usual FuSprGer 5. This was a FuSprGer 6, a link to battalion level with a voice range of 6km (3.73 miles). At a higher command level the *Panzerbefehlswagen 38(t)* (SdKfz 267) had the usual FuSprGer 5 plus a FuSprGer 8 and was fitted with a rigid frame aerial. The FuSprGer 8 had a maximum voice range of 10km (6.2 miles).

PzKpfw 38(t) Models

Ausf A. When the *Wehrmacht* marched into what was left of Czechoslovakia in March 1939 the first examples of the TNH-S were still incomplete. The Germans completed the first production batch with minimal modifications other than the provision of the standard German FuSprGer 5 radio mentioned above and the removal of some ammunition racks in the interior to provide more working space for the loader/radio operator. A total of 150 examples of this model were manufactured, including a batch of 37 basically similar vehicles purchased by Slovakia.

Ausf B. The production changes on this model compared to the Ausf A included revised external equipment stowage, the provision of *Notek* night driving lights and the fitting of German radio equipment. Some slight modifications were also introduced to the plate covering the gunner's sight. In total 110 tanks of this model were manufactured.

Ausf C. On this model the hull front armour was increased to 40mm (1.57in). The original rod aerial mounting was changed to a standard German pattern. In addition the exhaust muffler was moved to the top of the rear plate on many examples to allow room for a smoke-discharger to be fitted below. Production of this model was 150.

ABOVE: The left-side of the PzKpfw 38(t) *neue Art* reconnaissance tank. Comparison with the Ausf E/F opposite shows the main differences between the old and new designs – a new turret with a fixed cupola extended across the top. A more powerful engine was fitted requiring changes to the engine decking and a double exhaust system. *(VF)*

ABOVE AND RIGHT: These factory photographs show an Ausf E or F with a straight plate in front of the driver. Note that the ball mounting for the machine guns have been left in bare metal. In the upper photograph note the box for smoke grenades is now carried on the hull rear under the silencer. *(VF)*

133

LEFT: These battle-damaged PzKpfw 38(t)s are being repaired after capture by the Russians before being put back into service. The front tank is the command version Ausf F, distinguished by the plated-over hull machine gun aperture. The radio operator's visor has been replaced by a simple hinged plate. *(VF)*

ABOVE: An *Aufklärungspanzer 38(t) mit 2cm KwK 38 auf PzKpfw 38(t)* (reconnaissance tank) captured in Normandy, 1944. It is one of 70 built with the same gun turret as used on armoured cars. Since these were wider than standard turrets a complex new superstructure was designed. *(TG)*

Ausf D. This model was virtually identical to the Ausf C other than a splash protector for the turret ring was added. A total of 105 were manufactured.

Ausf E. With this model the hull and turret frontal armour thickness was increased to 50mm (1.97in) and those of the hull and turret sides to 30mm (1.18in). The previous 'stepped' plate in front of the driver's position was replaced by a flat plate as part of this process. The extra weight made the vehicle slightly nose heavy so the front suspension unit pairs were provided with an extra spring leaf. A total of 305 was produced.

Ausf F. With this model a bracket for seven spare track links on the lower front hull became a standard fitting. Extra fuel jerrican racks were added to the external stowage. In total, 250 were manufactured.

Ausf G. This was the last of the PzKpfw 38(t) light tank models to be manufactured and differed from the earlier models mainly in simplified construction methods. The front *Notek* light was moved to the upper edge of the hull front from the earlier position on the trackguard. It retained the full armour thicknesses of the late production models. Although 500 had been ordered only 306 were built. The remaining 194 chassis were completed as *Panzerjäger* (tank hunter).

ABOVE: The front of the *Aufklärungspanzer 38(t)* showing the overhang of the redesigned superstructure. Note that it is angled outward at the top and then inward at the bottom. This was to allow access to tools carried on the trackguards. *(TG)*

Ausf H and Ausf M. Chassis with these designations were manufactured exclusively for *Panzerjäger* or self-propelled artillery. On the Ausf H the gun was mounted forward while on the Ausf M it was at the rear, as the engine was moved to the left front. The engine, the Praga EPA AC, had a second carburettor fitted and the power output was increased to 150hp at 2,500rpm.

Ausf L. This front-engined model had an overhanging open superstructure at the rear to accommodate a 2cm Flak 38 air-defence cannon.

Ausf S. The Ausf S was a model anomaly originally ordered as the TNH-Sv light tank by Sweden but commandeered by the Germans while still on the production lines. It was basically similar to the Ausf C although the frontal armour was increased to 50mm (1.97in), the side armour remaining at 15mm (0.59in). Only 90 of this model were manufactured, many being passed to the Slovak Free State.

It should be stressed that during rebuilds and overhauls many later modifications were added to earlier models so it is difficult to provide sound recognition points to visually differentiate between each model. In addition many units added their own stowage and/or other modifications.

ABOVE: The very last production Ausf G at the factory, 2 June 1942. At this time the *Notek* blackout driving light had been removed. *(VF)*

LEFT: The same tank: note the half-round covers for the track tension adjusters as well as the final position of the silencer over the smoke grenade box. Note that the two pickaxes are not stowed flat against the superstructure side, but rest at an angle. *(VF)*

RIGHT: An Ausf G in postwar Czech army service. It was designated the LT38. The new national emblem is on the turret side, but the absence of a serial number means that the photograph was taken before these were allocated in 1946. The colour scheme appears to be overall khaki paint as used on Czech equipment after World War Two. *(VF)*

Chapter 3

Armament

A Škoda anti-tank gun was selected for the new LTvz.38 and continued in use for the PzKpfw 38(t). Although good against thin armour of other light tanks it was outclassed by thicker enemy armour .

For its era the PzKpfw 38(t) was a well-armed light tank. The main armament was a hard-hitting 37mm high-velocity gun and this was coupled with two machine guns, one co-axial.

Good as this armament may have been in 1939, by 1941 increases in enemy tank armour had degraded the main gun's capabilities to the point where it no longer had a viable front line career.

Armament

Before 1919 Škoda had supplied all the artillery needs of the old Austro-Hungarian armies and went on to do the same for the new Czechoslovakia. Its output ranged from heavy artillery to anti-aircraft guns although it was rather slow in the development of anti-tank guns. The first Škoda anti-tank gun did not appear until 1933. Known as the A2 L/25 it had a calibre of 47mm but it did not progress very far as Škoda turned its attentions to the then fashionable 37mm (1.456in) calibre, finally producing the A4 (in-service designation was SU vz.34 [SU – *Utocna Vozba* – armoured vehicles]) that armed the Czech Army's LT vz.35 tanks. The gun proved generally unsatisfactory in the tank armament role as its anti-armour performance was indifferent. Its recoil brake and recuperator cylinders also protruded beyond the gun mantlet and were therefore vulnerable to damage from incoming fire.

Škoda sought to correct these shortcomings with a further series of designs, one of which was selected to arm the TNH light tank series. This was the Škoda 37mm A7, based on the in-service towed KPUV vz.34. The monobloc barrel of what became the UV vz.38 was approximately 47.8 calibres long and was designed from the outset with the recoil mechanisms behind the protection afforded by the turret and mantlet armour. The vertical sliding block breech was semi-automatic, opening to eject the spent case as the gun returned to battery after recoil, the spent case from the one-piece round falling into a canvas bag under the breech. This system permitted a rate of fire with a trained crew of 15 rounds per minute (rpm). On the TNH-S/PzKpfw 38(t) the gun had a full 360° traverse, an elevation of +25° and a depression of -10°.

ABOVE: The co-axial machine gun has a cradle with slots to allow cooling, though most PzKpfw 38(t)s used an armoured cradle with solid sides. Both the machine gun and main gun have the ends of the barrels temporarily sealed. The hull machinegun is completely covered against damp and dust. *(TM)*

Ammunition stowage was provided for 72 rounds, half of them arranged in easy access racks located in the turret bustle and the rest retained in ammunition boxes stowed around the fighting compartment interior.

The first armour-piercing (AP) round fired from the UV vz.38 weighed 1.47kg (3.24lb) of which the solid hardened-steel projectile weighed 850g (1.87lb). Having a nominal muzzle velocity of 750m/sec (2,460ft/sec) the projectile could penetrate 35mm (1.378in) of armour at 500m (547yd). This round was known in German service as the 3.7cm Pzgr 37(t) (Pzgr – *Panzergranate*).

This armour penetration capability was regarded as more than satisfactory when the gun was introduced into service but soon after the UV vz.38 had become the 3.7cm KwK 38(t) (KwK – *KampfwagenKanone* – combat vehicle/tank gun) in German hands it was regarded as inadequate against the emerging generation of armoured vehicles. A more powerful AP round was therefore introduced during 1941 in an attempt to prolong the viable service life of the gun. The new round was of a type known as the AP40 (Pzgr 40[t] see table on page 38) and differed from the conventional solid projectiles of the time by having a smaller, lighter yet dense penetrator core. This core was carried within the mild steel projectile body and behind a light alloy ballistic shield. The core was formed from a tungsten carbide alloy with better armour penetration capabilities than the conventional steel projectiles. As the projectile weighed only 368g (0.81lb) it could be fired at a muzzle velocity of 1,040m/sec (3,412ft/sec), enabling the core to penetrate 64mm (2.52in) of armour at 100m (109yd). However, as the projectile was light its velocity soon fell away so that at 500m (547yd) the penetration was degraded to just 34mm (1.34in).

There was another drawback with the AP40 round, one shared with all the tungsten-cored rounds developed for German anti-armour guns. The core had to be manufactured using imported wolfram (there were only two limited-capacity wolfram mines within Germany). Wolfram forms the raw material source for tungsten powder, as used in the AP40 cores, and was soon in very short supply due

LEFT: The main gun cradle with the gun removed. The elevation hand-wheel with firing trigger are at the left and the cable for the semi-automatic breech mechanism is below. The manual breech operating lever used in emergencies can be seen above the cable, with the clamp for the breech mechanism in front. *(TM)*

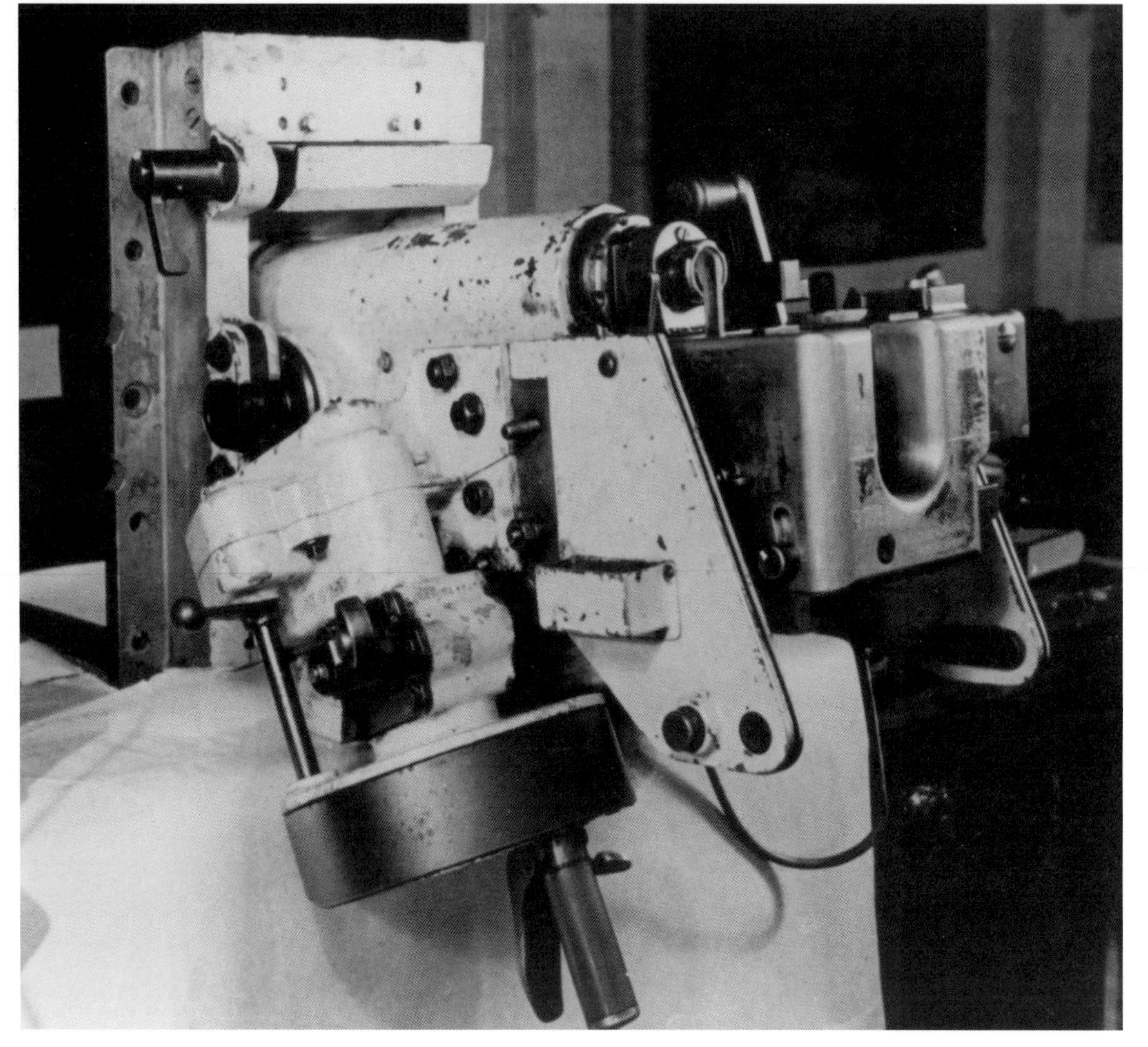

LEFT: The complete gun, mount and frontal armour have been removed for examination. The gun cradle, elevation hand-wheel and mechanism are clearly shown, together with the firing trigger on the handwheel and the recoil shields either side of the breech. *(TM)*

RIGHT: The dismounted gun shows the recoil guide on the top surface and the breech operating mechanism's enclosure on the side. Manufacturing and acceptance marks on the breech show that this gun was produced in 1940. *(TM)*

RIGHT: The manual operating lever for the breech is on top of the mechanism box and the cable for semi-automatic operation below. *(TM)*

ABOVE: The top of the gun mantlet on an Ausf E or F. Note that although the recoil cylinder and the sides of the mount are armoured there is no protection against bullet splash for the top of the mantlet. *(AN)*

to the Allied naval blockade of Germany. The point was reached where all available stocks of refined tungsten had to be conserved for machine tools, without which the German war economy could not function. Production of Pzgr 40(t) rounds was therefore soon terminated and rounds already manufactured were carefully set aside for only the most pressing combat needs.

This situation can be seen in the production totals for 3.7cm KwK 38(t) armour-penetrating ammunition:

	1939	1940	1941	1942	1943
Pzgr 37(t)					
	132,100	1,137,000	649,900	205,700	1,500
Pzgr 40(t)					
	-	-	603,300	173,900	-

The UV vz.38 gun also fired a high-explosive (HE) projectile weighing 825g (1.82lb), the complete round weighing 1.42kg (3.13lb). Fired at a muzzle velocity of 730m/sec (2,395ft/sec) and with the barrel at an elevation angle of +5° the maximum range was 4,000m (4,375yd), although combat ranges would have been much shorter than that because the sighting telescope was only calibrated for ranges up to 2,000m (2,180yd).

To simplify matters at a time when the ex-Czech tanks and their guns were urgently needed, German ordnance staff retained the Škoda gun and its ammunition in production, without any changes, to suit their normally strictly-applied specifications. Thereby arose a difficulty as the gun and its ammunition differed from other similar calibre guns. Its calibre was actually 37.2mm (1.465in), the minute difference meaning that German 37mm ammunition could not be fired from the Czech gun, while the cartridge case had a marginally different profile. Needless to say this differing ammunition situation imposed a more complicated logistical load on already well-stretched supply services, so in a few cases the Škoda gun was replaced during rebuilds by its standard German equivalent, the Rheinmetall-Borsig 3.7cm KwK L/46.5.

The Škoda and German guns were almost identical ballistically although the muzzle velocity of the German gun was slightly lower at 745m/sec (2,444ft/sec). When this was coupled with a conventional armour-piercing projectile weighing 685g (1.51lb) the armour penetration performance was 29mm (1.14in) at 500m (547yd). AP40 pattern ammunition also became available for the German gun but it suffered from the same long-range performance fall-off properties and supply availability as other similar ammunition types in German service.

Specification

Škoda A7/(3.7cm KwK 38[t])

Calibre:	37.2mm	
Length:	1.778m (70in)	
Projectile weight:		
	(AP)	850g (1.87lb)
	(AP40)	368g (0.81lb)
	(HE)	825g (1.82lb)
Depression on vehicle:		-10^{0}
Elevation on vehicle:		$+25^{0}$
Traverse on vehicle:		360^{0}
Muzzle velocity:		
	(AP)	750m/sec (2,460ft/sec)
	(AP40)	1,040m/sec (3,412ft/sec)
	(HE)	730m/sec (2,395ft/sec)
Max range:	(HE)	4,000m (4,375yd) at elevation of $+5^{0}$
Max effective range:		
	(AP)	900m (984yd)
Armour penetration:		
	(AP)	35mm (1.378in) at 500m (547yd)
	(AP40)	34mm (1.34in) at 500m (547yd)

Machine Guns

When Czechoslovakia was first formed its main machine gun legacy from the old Empire was 4,773 *Schwarzlose* water-cooled machine guns that, thanks to their water-cooled barrels, proved unsuitable for armoured vehicle applications. By 1923 the firm of *Československa Zbrojovka Brno* (ZB) had been established at Brno with Václav Holek as head designer. From the ZB design bureau came numerous advanced machine gun designs, including the ZB vz.26 that was destined to be looked upon as one of the best light machine guns ever created.

RIGHT: A comparison of a ZB vz.37 machine gun, on the right, with the British BESA (a licence-built version) on the left. Both have the receiver covers open to show the bullet. Note the BESA has a single pistol grip while the ZB vz.37 has two grips and cooling fins on the barrel. *(TM)*

LEFT: The ZB vz.37 and complete mount. The turret front plate was in two main sections. Note the stop on the side, this prevented the machine gun from firing at the main gun barrel when operated independently. *(TM)*

From 1930 onwards ZB also turned its attentions to a heavy machine gun adaptable not just for ground mountings but also for fortification, air defence and armoured vehicle roles. After some abortive developments the ZB vz.37 emerged and was eventually selected to be the co-axial and hull machine gun for the TNH series and all its subsequent light tank models.

The 7.92mm ZB vz.37 was a gas-operated, belt-fed machine gun with a heavy finned barrel. Ammunition was fed in 100 or 200 round metal link belts and it was possible to select one of two rates of fire. When used as an air defence weapon the cyclic rate could be 750rpm but for ground targets it was 550rpm. In addition two round weights were available with different muzzle velocities: 880m/sec for the light round and 780m/sec for the heavy, the heavy bullet intended to be fired to the longer ranges and for light armour penetration. Spent cases were ejected into a cloth bag below the gun. Ammunition stowage inside the vehicle was up to 2,700 rounds although this was often reduced to provide more internal space for the crew.

When installed in the TNH-S/PzKpfw 38(t) the hull gun was placed in a ball mounting that could be fixed or flexible according to who was operating the gun. When fired by the driver it was fixed so that fire struck the ground 300m (328yd) directly in front of the vehicle. A very flimsy ring sight was mounted in front of the driver's vision port to assist aiming when in this mode but its hinged mount, intended for it to be swung down when not needed, was vulnerable to breakage and it was removed in many cases. The more usual firing mode was with the gun using its flexible ball mounting to full advantage. In this mode the gunner was the radio operator/loader using a x2.6 telescopic sight calibrated to a range of 1,500m (1,640yd). Barrel elevation and depression were both 10^0 and the traverse 28^0.

The co-axial machine gun moved with the turret and main armament barrel so it had a full 360^0 traverse, an elevation of $+25^0$ and a depression of -10^0. It could also be disconnected from the main gun to be aimed and fired by the loader. The co-axial installation had two shortcomings. One was that access for reloading by the commander was difficult to the extent that the already busy loader had to undertake the task. Another problem was that over certain sectors of the turret traverse the hanging ammunition belt could create difficulties for the driver. Should the optical sights for either machine gun become unusable a steel plug could be removed from the mounting to reveal rudimentary iron sights.

For the Germans the ZB vz.53 became the 7.92mm MG 37(t). When placed on a tripod and with a heavier barrel than that employed on armoured vehicles (to permit greater volumes of sustained fire) the machine gun was usually issued to the *Waffen SS* or second-line units. The British also used the ZB vz.37 with their tanks, a manufacturing licence having been obtained by

RIGHT: The inside detail of the turret machine gun's ball mount. On the right side, by the ball, is the handle of the lock that held it co-axial to the main gun when not wanted for independent fire. The mount for the sighting telescope used for independent fire can be seen but the telescope has been removed. *(TM)*

BSA during 1936. To the British the ZB vz.37 was known as the Besa, still firing 7.92mm ammunition instead of the British 0.303in.

For the record, the ZB vz.37 was 1.095m (43.1in) long, the barrel being 733mm (28.85in) in length. Weight as an armoured vehicle gun was 18.88kg (41.62lb). The rimless cartridge fired was the same 7.92mm Mauser cartridge as used by the German armed forces. Ammunition was carried in nine boxes each containing 300 rounds.

By the time that the first *Marder III* (tank hunter) on the front-engined Ausf M chassis appeared the German ordnance supply system had started to issue the 7.92mm MG 34 to replace the Czech machine gun, a practice continued on all subsequent variants. The air-cooled MG 34 had a cyclic fire rate of 900rpm. For local and close defence the *Marder III* and later PzKpfw 38(t) variants were meant to carry one or two 9mm sub-machine guns (officially a 9mm MP 40 but often something else) together with 192 or 384 rounds of 9mm ammunition.

Variant Vehicle Guns

To complete this short account of PzKpfw 38(t) armament a brief outline of the guns carried on the *Panzerjäger* and self-propelled artillery variants is provided below:

Gun	7.62cm PaK 36(r)	7.5cm PaK 40/3	7.5cm PaK 39	15cm sIG 33/1
Bore	7.62cm (3in)	7.5cm	7.5cm	14.91cm
Length of gun barrel (calibres)	54	46	48	11.4
Length	3.898m (153.5in)	3.7m (145.7in)	3.7m(145.7in)	1.7m (66.9in)
Length of rifling	2.93m (115.35in)	2.461m (96.9in)	2.461m (96.9in)	1.346m (53in)
Projectile weight (AP)	7.54kg (16.62lb)	6.8kg (15lb)	6.8kg (15lb)	(HE)38kg (83.8lb)
Depression on vehicle	-8°	-5°	-6°	-3°
Elevation on vehicle	+13.5°	+13°	+12°	+72°
Traverse	42°	42°	5° l, 10°r	10°
Muzzle velocity	740m/sec (2,428ft/sec)	792m/sec (2,600ft/sec)	792m/sec (2,600ft/sec)	240m/sec (790ft/sec)
Armour penetration at 500m (547yd)	120mm (4.72in)	135mm (5.315in)	135mm (5.315in)	n/a

* PaK – *PanzerabwehrKanone* (tank gun)

Chapter 4
In Service

Although classed as a light tank the LT vz.38 and PzKpfw 38(t) were a match in most respects for the German PzKpfw III medium tank.

Most of the PzKpfw 38(t) tanks available for the invasion of Poland, about 100, were allocated to the 67th *PanzerAbteilung* (battalion), which was part of the 3rd *Leichte* (Light) Division. They fought their way through the Polish defences to a point south of Warsaw, and then helped to defeat a Polish counter-attack to the west of Warsaw. Several of their tanks were knocked out during the fighting, but all were recovered and repaired. After the Polish campaign the 3rd *Leichte* Division was converted into a full Panzer Division, the 8th, and received more PzKpfw 38(t)s from new production to equip its 10th Panzer Regiment.

Following the fall of Poland the heyday of the PzKpfw 38(t) was perhaps the campaign against France during May and June of 1940.

It was then deployed in two Panzer Divisions, the 7th and 8th, which could field 230 vehicles between them (including command vehicles). These formations easily overcame Belgian and Luxembourgois resistance respectively and crossed the French frontier. They moved rapidly across Northern France from the crossing of the Meuse onwards until they reached the Channel coast, completely bypassing and demoralising static French units in the field as they went. About 50 PzKpfw 38(t)s were knocked out in this campaign, but nearly all were repairable.

The 8th Panzers took part in the April 1941 campaign in Yugoslavia but the main emphasis that year was the invasion of the Soviet Union on 22 June 1941 and the battle that followed. Nearly 700 PzKpfw 38(t)s were with the Panzer Divisions by 1941, with about 100 in reserve. They equipped five out of the 17 Panzer Divisions involved in Operation Barbarossa (7th, 8th, 12th, 19th and 20th). The 8th Panzer Division took part in the amazingly fast advances through the Baltic States and was then sent to join the other divisions that had advanced almost as quickly through Russia, surrounding and capturing large numbers of Soviet troops in major battles. Despite these successes they were unable to stand up to the Russian T-34 and KV-1 tanks with their heavier armour and better guns, only overcoming them because the Russian tankers had poor vision devices so could be outmanoeuvred and outfought. The Russians also had few spare parts to deal with mechanical malfunctions, and probably lost more tanks due to

ABOVE: A PzKpfw 38(t) Ausf A with the original Czech armoured radio antenna mounted above the track-guard. The large turret numbers are typical of the 7th Panzer Division, but no unit markings can be seen as confirmation. *(TM)*

this than through battle damage. The PzKpfw 38(t)s eventually reached the outskirts of Moscow, where ice, snow and the stubborn Russian defence halted them.

A further PzKfpw 38(t) division, the 22nd, reached the Eastern Front during February 1942. By then the PzKpfw 38(t) was becoming increasingly outclassed in almost every way, from armoured protection to firepower, by the ever increasing numbers of Soviet Army T-34 and KV-1 tanks. Nevertheless production of the vehicle as a light tank continued until June 1942, by which time increasing consideration was being given to employing the chassis as a self-propelled anti-tank gun platform. These were the *Panzerjäger*, of which more elsewhere. Battle weary PzKpfw 38(t)s were gradually withdrawn during 1942 as front line vehicles, only to be virtually rebuilt in most cases, usually by BMM, and prepared for conversion to new forms.

The PzKpfw 38(t) was therefore gradually removed from Panzer operations and ended its days as a light tank by forming part of the anti-Partisan demountable defences of some of the armoured railway trains that saw extensive service on the Eastern Front. Approximately 150 PzKpfw 38(t)s remained in depots and training establishments as late as March 1945 and may well have been thrust into the last desperate defence of Germany, though no records remain as proof of this happening.

Much of the success of the PzKpfw 38(t) during the early war years could be allocated to its all-round and reliable automotive performance, two features often displayed during the break out and following phases of the invasions of Poland, France and the Soviet Union. The results could be spectacular when these valuable assets were combined with the organisational and rapid response procedures employed by German tank formation commanders, especially as seen in France during May and June 1940. During that campaign the PzKpfw 38(t) was frequently potentially outclassed by the opposing Allied armour but overcame such difficulties by aggressive and determined moves that by-passed and isolated the opposition. Yet it has to be repeated that by late 1941 the PzKpfw 38(t) was no longer effective as a front line light tank.

LEFT: A scene from early in the Russian campaign. The column has halted while fighting rages ahead. Note the great amount of kit carried on the engine deck of the tanks, needed because supply trucks could not keep up with the rapid advance of the armoured columns. *(TM)*

LEFT: The white turret number, a large 1 and small 3, shows that this is a command tank of a Panzer battalion. The crew appear to have added a rack to the back of the turret to carry extra ammunition boxes. The unit symbol in front of the number is that of the 20th Panzer Division and is painted in yellow. *(AN)*

ABOVE: This photograph was taken near Smolensk and shows petrol drums being delivered by rail so that the tanks can be refuelled. The tank is probably an Ausf C or D. *(AN)*

RIGHT: A damaged Ausf G; note at least one penetration of the armour is visible, also there are two shell holes in the wheels. The German cross on the back of the turret is unusual but no unit markings are visible. *(AN)*

LEFT: Captured PzKpfz 38(t)s being rebuilt by Russian mechanics in May 1942. The yellow unit symbol below the cross on the nearer tank is that of the 19th Panzer Division but the tiny swastika on the cross and the code above have been applied by the Russians. *(AN)*

ABOVE: Russian tank crewmen checking a captured Ausf C or D. The single-digit turret number is unusual and a large stowage bin has been added above the trackguard. *(AN)*

LEFT: A captured Ausf C or D is being inspected by a Russian soldier. The original caption notes that it was disabled by a direct hit from artillery and will be melted down as scrap. *(AN)*

ABOVE: A captured Panzer 38(t) Ausf E or F. The turret is that of an Ausf E or F but the engine deck is earlier, so this tank had probably been re-built at the factory before capture. *(TM)*

RIGHT: The Swiss LTH (right). For some reason the turret hatches are transposed so that the cupola is on the left. The LT vz.35 tanks in the background appear to be in Czech pre-war camouflage, though the turret numbers are not standard for Czech service. *(AN)*

Chapter 5

Variants

Although the PzKpfw 38(t) was obsolete by 1942 the chassis was so reliable that it formed the basis for many other vehicles – self-propelled artillery, anti-tank guns and Flak tanks.

While the PzKpfw 38(t) light tanks were important military assets for Germany during 1939 and 1940, by the end of the following year their value as combat machines had been much degraded. Despite the addition of extra armour on the later production vehicles they became more and more vulnerable to the new generation of tank and anti-tank guns while at the same time their main 37mm gun armament proved to be increasingly ineffective, especially against Soviet tanks such as the T-34 series.

New Employments

There was no way the PzKpfw 38(t) turret could be enlarged to accommodate a heavier calibre gun, as its turret ring diameter was limited by the width of its hull and a larger gun demanded a larger turret ring. (A subsequent 1944 Krupp project to graft a lightened PzKpfw IV tank turret armed with a 7.5 cm KwK 43 L/48 gun onto a PzKpfw 38[t] hull with the intention of rapidly producing an economically manufactured combat tank was soon abandoned as impractical.)

That did not mean that the days of the PzKpfw 38(t) were over – far from it. From 1942 onwards the basic chassis and hull of the TNH-S were adapted in numerous ways to supply a variety of needs. It can safely be stated that the TNH-S/PzKpfw 38(t) chassis became an even more important asset within the German armoured vehicle inventory as a chassis for other vehicles than it had been as a light tank.

The first use of the chassis was one improvised measure amongst many others intended to counter the ever-increasing numbers of Soviet tanks encountered on the Eastern Front. Defeating the thick armour of the Soviet T-34 and KV-1 tanks called for a high-velocity gun firing a kinetic-energy projectile with a calibre of at least 75mm. During late 1941 and early 1942 the only German guns of this nature were the towed 7.5cm PaK 40 and the tank 7.5cm KwK 40 earmarked for the PzKpfw IV series, both only just entering series production by Rheinmetall-Borsig at Unterlüss and elsewhere. At that time the demands for this gun were so pressing that none was available for the self-propelled

ABOVE: A *Panzerjäger 38(t) für 7.62cm PaK 36(r)*, or *Marder III* of the first type with a captured Russian gun. This scene during trials or training shows just how high the silhouette was, and difficult to conceal from the enemy. *(T&A)*

role, even though the need for such a weapon was well appreciated by German ordnance planners.

Self-propelled anti-tank guns were by early 1942 known as *Panzerjäger* or tank hunters (the nearest Allied equivalent term was tank destroyer). They were not normally a component of the Panzer divisions, but did serve in *Panzerjäger* companies within some Panzer formations. *Panzerjäger* guns had limited traverse mountings with limited frontal and side protection, and little or none to the rear. As they were only intended as mobile anti-tank gun platforms their combat function was either to stalk enemy tanks or to ambush them from behind cover, and then to get away as rapidly as possible before retaliation arrived. They did so as part of the armament of infantry and *Panzergrenadier* (mechanised infantry) divisions.

The discovery of the Soviet tank hordes that faced German forces meant that the calls for adequately-gunned *Panzerjäger* became increasingly strident. As it would take time to develop a dedicated vehicle for this role the way was open for an array of German improvisations to plug the gaps. The calls came at a time when production of the PzKpfw 38(t) as a light tank was just about to cease, so its chassis came under active consideration as a *Panzerjäger* platform. The problem then was to find a suitable gun because the Rheinmetall-Borsig weapon was still in short supply.

As far as the PzKpfw 38(t) story was concerned the gun answer came from the Eastern Front in the form of war booty. During the early stages of the German invasion of the Soviet Union from June 1941 onwards huge masses of Soviet equipment fell into German hands virtually intact, among the spoils being hundreds of 76.2mm (3in) 76-36 field guns. These long-barrelled towed guns already had a more than adequate capability as anti-tank weapons, but by reconfiguring the chamber and firing suitably modified 7.5cm PaK 40 ammunition the gun could deliver an even better anti-armour performance. It then became capable of firing a 7.54kg (16.62lb) projectile that could penetrate 120mm (4.72in) of armour at 500m (547yd). The muzzle velocity was 740m/sec (2,428ft/sec). Once converted the gun then became the 7.62cm PaK 36, later regarded as

ABOVE: An early production *Marder III Ausf M.* Only a few vehicles were built with the exhaust pipe running inside the fighting compartment to where it can just be seen exiting from the rear plate under the silencer. Most *Marder III Ausf M* vehicles had the exhaust pipe led through the side grille and along the outside of the fighting compartment. *(TM)*

LEFT: A *Marder III Ausf M.* Note the extensively-riveted construction of the fighting compartment sides and the gunshield. *(TM)*

being one of the best all-round anti-tank weapons produced between 1939 and 1945. So many of these guns were readily available to the Germans that they were obvious candidates for the *Panzerjäger* role so they were soon combined with the PzKpfw 38(t) chassis.

Converting the light tank to a *Panzerjäger* was comparatively simple and was accomplished using both retired and new-production chassis. The turret and forward superstructure roof were removed and a cruciform base for the gun mount was placed in the previous position of the turret. A thin armoured superstructure was built on top of the front and sides of the original hull to protect the crew. Ammunition stowage in the vehicle was provided for 30 rounds plus a further 1,200 rounds for the machine gun. As these early *Panzerjäger* were somewhat hasty conversions they retained the original ZB vz.53 hull machine gun.

This improvisation was known as the *Panzerjäger 38(t) für 7.62cm PaK 36(r)* (SdKfz 139), although this cumbersome designation was often changed to *Marder III* (Marten III) to simplify matters (*Marder I* and *Marder II* had been used to designate conversions on other chassis). A batch of 66 was sent to the *Afrika Korps* out of the first vehicles delivered.

This vehicle/gun combination was so successful that Hitler himself issued an edict that all PzKpfw 38(t) production would from then onwards be used only for self-propelled weapon purposes. Following that edict the numbers of TNH-S related vehicle types emerging from BMM proliferated.

By October 1942 a total of 344 *Marder III* with 7.62cm guns had been delivered, with a further 19 converted from old PzKpfw 38(t) during 1943. The turrets and armament from these and other similar conversions were allocated to the *Atlantikwall* or other fixed defences, at least 350 turrets being so employed.

By late 1942 there were sufficient 7.5cm PaK 40 guns available for them to be fitted on the production lines in place of the ex-Soviet guns, the result becoming the *Panzerjäger 38(t) für 7.5cm PaK 40/3* (SdKfz 138), confusingly also designated the *Marder III*. At least 275 examples of this vehicle were manufactured from new while a further 336 were converted from redundant light tanks during 1943. Eighteen examples were delivered to the Slovak Army during 1944. On-board ammunition

BELOW LEFT: A captured standard production *Marder III Ausf M. (TM)*

BELOW RIGHT: A captured *Marder III Ausf M*, showing a typical way of stowing the tow cables. Note the exhaust pipe coming round the right corner of the superstructure. *(TM)*

Marder III (Marten) (SdKfz 139)	
Crew	four
Combat weight, nominal	10,670kg (23,523lb)
Length with gun	5.85m (19.2ft)
Width	2.16m (7.08ft)
Height	2.5m (8.2ft)
Track width	293mm (11.7in)
Max road speed	47km/h (29.2mph)
Gradient	30°
Vertical obstacle	850mm (33.7in)
Trench crossing	1.8m (5.9ft)
Fording	900mm (3.0ft)
Fuel capacity, total	320 litres (70.4 gallons)
Road range	185km (114.9 miles)
Engine	7,754cc Praga EPA AC six-cylinder in-line water-cooled petrol engine developing 130hp at 2,500rpm
Armament	one 7.62cm PaK 36(r) one 7.92mm MG 37(t)
AP projectile weight	7.54kg (16.42lb)
Barrel traverse	21° left, 21° right
Barrel elevation	-8° to +13°
Ammunition, 7.62cm	38 rounds
Ammunition, 7.92mm	600 rounds

Marder III (Marten) (Ausf H)	
Crew	four
Combat weight, nominal	10,800kg (23,810lb)
Length with gun	5.77m (18.9ft)
Width	2.15m (7.11ft)
Height	2.51m (8.235ft)
Track width	293mm (11.7in)
Max road speed	47km/h (29.2mph)
Gradient	30°
Vertical obstacle	800mm (31.7in)
Trench crossing	2.1m (7.0ft)
Fording	900mm (3.0ft)
Fuel capacity, total	320 litres (70.4 gallons)
Road range	240km (149.1 miles)
Engine	7,754cc Praga EPA AC six-cylinder in-line water-cooled petrol engine developing 150hp at 2,500rpm
Armament	one 7.5cm PaK 40/3 one 7.92mm MG 37(t)
AP projectile weight	6.8kg (15lb)
Barrel traverse	21° left, 21° right
Barrel elevation	-8° to +13°
Ammunition, 7.5cm	38 rounds
Ammunition, 7.92mm	600 rounds

RIGHT: *Marder III Ausf H* fresh from the factory. The large sliding armour plate protecting the gunsight aperture is partly open, showing the upper rail on which it slid. The lower rail is hidden behind the plate so can only be seen when it is slid shut. The driver's compartment of the Ausf H was that of the original PzKpfw 38 (t) riveted from plates with a flat front. *(TM)*

BELOW RIGHT: The same *Marder III Ausf H*. Note the position of the radio antenna on top of the side armour. Behind is the crosswise tubular support for a canvas weather cover over the fighting compartment. *(TM)*

stowage was increased to 38 75mm rounds while 600 machine gun rounds were provided. On these vehicles the hull machine gun was still the ZB vz.53.

While successful in their intended combat mission both these models of the *Marder III* did have disadvantages. With their guns and crew perched over the chassis they were vulnerable to side and top attack from artillery projectiles and small arms, to say nothing of the elements. In addition they were high vehicles that were difficult to conceal. A further drawback in production terms was that they were rather expensive to manufacture, much of the internal space being unused. There was one way of rectifying these shortcomings and that was to move the engine compartment to the left front of the vehicle alongside the driver to create the Ausf M chassis. The gun mounting and its protection were then moved to a new, lower position overhanging the rear of the hull. This relocation provided both the gun and crew with four-sided all-round protection, although the top remained open. (The combat area could be covered by a canvas awning for weather protection.) The result was the *Panzerjäger 38(t) für 7.5cm PaK 40/3 Ausf M* (SdKfz 138), still known as the *Marder III*. This model was awarded a high production priority with 975 produced between April 1943 and May 1944. Production was only terminated in favour of the *Jagdpanzer 38*, of which more later.

The reduced internal volume of the rear-mounted combat compartment of the *Marder III* limited the number of 7.5cm rounds carried to 27. This vehicle was the first to utilise the 7.92mm MG 34 in place of the Czech ZB vz.53, ammunition stowage for this gun being 1,500 rounds. One or two sub-machine guns for local defence were also added from this variant onwards.

There were plans to mount a 7.5 cm KwK 42 L/70 tank gun in a suitably modified *Marder III* but this project did not get past the model stage.

Marder III (Marten) (Ausf M)

Crew	four
Combat weight, nominal	10,150kg (22,376lb)
Length with gun	5.02m (16.47ft)
Width	2.135m (8.63ft)
Height	2.35m (7.712ft)
Track width	293mm (11.7in)
Max road speed	47km/h (29.2mph)
Gradient	30°
Vertical obstacle	800mm (31.7in)
Trench crossing	2.1m (7.0ft)
Fording	900mm (3.0ft)
Fuel capacity, total	320 litres (70.4 gallons)
Road range	200km (155.3 miles)
Engine	7,754cc Praga EPA AC six-cylinder in-line water-cooled petrol engine developing 150hp at 2,500rpm
Armament	one 7.5cm PaK 40/3 one 7.92mm MG 34
AP projectile weight	6.8kg (15lb)
Barrel traverse	21° left, 21° right
Barrel elevation	-8° to +13°
Ammunition, 7.5cm	27 rounds
Ammunition, 7.92mm	1,500 rounds

LEFT: A *Marder III Ausf H*. The stowage bracket on the side armour was not seen on *Marders* on the battlefield. *(VF)*

BELOW LEFT: A *Marder III Ausf M.* Note how very different the superstructure became when the engine was moved to the middle of the vehicle. *(VF)*

RIGHT: A *Marder III Ausf H* being loaded for transport from the factory. *(VF)*

BELOW: A *Panzerjäger 38(t) für 7.62cm PaK 36(r)* at the factory. *(VF)*

ABOVE: A *Marder III Ausf H* camouflaged with tree branches, a common practice in wooded areas. A tactical number is partly visible under the branches. Note how the ammunition was stowed inside the side armour plates. *(TG)*

LEFT: A 15cm sIG 31/1 *Grille* Ausf M heavy infantry support gun shows a different attempt at concealment with logs and broken baulks of timber leant against the vehicle to break up the outline when seen from the air. The photograph was taken in Italy. *(T&A)*

RIGHT: Commonwealth troops are examining a captured *Marder III Ausf H*. Unfortunately no markings are visible, but close inspection reveals that this *Marder* has been given a roughly applied coat of *Zimmerit* anti-magnetic-mine paste by the crew. *Zimmerit* was never applied to the *Marder* at the factory, and normally was only supplied to tank units for self-application in the field. *(T&A)*

RIGHT: A captured *Marder III Ausf H* has been put back into use by the British. It is one of the very rare early *Marder* with the exhaust pipe exiting through the rear plate. Note also the equally rare rear mud-guards that were only fitted to very early vehicles. *(TM)*

LEFT: A knocked-out *Marder III Ausf H* near Esperia in the Cassino area of Italy, 1943. It is unusual in carrying full markings including the Division symbol and the anti-tank unit symbol. The Division sign is that of *71. Infanterie Division* denoting it as a *Marder* of *Panzerjäger Abteilung 171*, the Division's anti-tank unit. *(TM)*

BELOW: A unit of *Panzerjäger 38(t) für 7.62cm PaK 36(r)* at a railway station on the Russian Front. From the clean condition it can be assumed that this is a delivery of new equipment from the factory. One *Panzerjäger* has been unloaded already, and the others are on the flatcars in the background. *(AN)*

More SPs

The PzKpfw 38(t) chassis was not used just as a carrier for anti-tank guns. Once the initial pressing needs for *Panzerjäger* had been partially met consideration could be given to carrying the 15cm sIG 33/1 (sIG – *schwere InfanterieGeschütz*) heavy infantry gun to act as an artillery close fire support platform for mechanised infantry units. This was accomplished in much the same manner as with the 7.62cm PaK 36 (SdKfz 139) although the constructed results were somewhat cruder, even if the protective side plates did extend to the rear of the chassis. This vehicle was the *15cm sIG 33/1(Sfl) auf PzKpfw 38(t) Ausf H Grille* (Cricket) (SdKfz 138/1). It was effective enough in its intended fire support role yet only 200 were manufactured during 1943, followed by a second batch of 10, before production switched to the Ausf M chassis layout with the gun compartment positioned at the rear, as with the *Marder III.* Only 167 vehicles of this type, the *15cm sIG 33/1(Sfl) auf PzKpfw 38(t) Ausf K Grille* (SdKfz 138/1), were manufactured, the last during March 1945 after a long break to allow priority for the production of *Jagdpanzer 38(t).*

Both models of *Grille* had only limited on-board ammunition capacity (15 rounds) so to enable the vehicles to remain effective in the field for as long as possible a total of 103 *Munitionspanzer 38(t) (Sfl) auf PzKpfw 38(t)* (SdKfz 138/1) were produced. Of these 19 were built with the engine at the rear (the Ausf H chassis), with the remainder on the Ausf M chassis with the engine at the left front. These ammunition carriers were identical to the *Grille* but lacked the gun and its mounting, the barrel elevation slot being plated over. Racks holding 40 rounds occupied the internal area so the defensive armament was limited to the 7.92mm MG 34 machine gun in the hull front. It was planned that there would be two *Munitions-panzer 38(t)* for every six *Grille.*

Another weapon carrier built on a modified Ausf M chassis was the *Flakpanzer 38(t) auf Selbstfahrlafette 38(t) Ausf L* (SdKfz 140), another makeshift measure, this time to provide air defence for mechanised units in the field. The armour protection for the gun compartment ➤ page 67

LEFT: This *Grille Ausf H* was captured from the 2nd Panzer Division in Normandy. The camouflage is irregular rectangles and triangles in green over the dark yellow base coat. The Division's trident emblem is shown on the front left side and left rear door together with the tactical sign for a self-propelled artillery unit. The letter D on the left front plate appears to be black but the German cross on the side only shows faintly through the green paint. *(TM)*

LEFT: The other side of the same *Grille*. The only markings seen in view are German crosses on the side and the rear plate. The silencer is worth notice by modellers, showing the original camouflage paint instead of the rust that is usually assumed to replace all paint after a few hours of engine running. *(TM)*

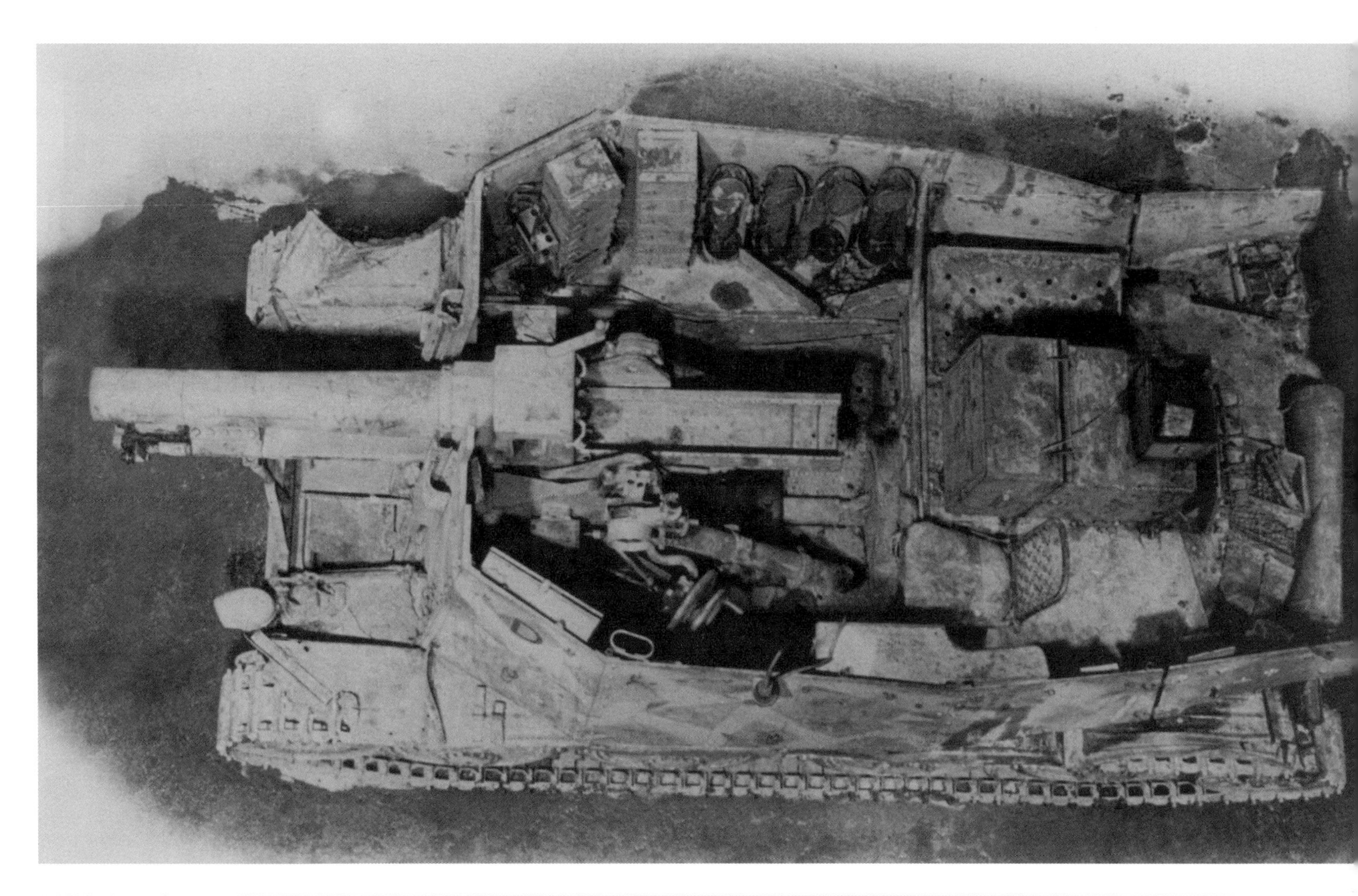

ABOVE: A good overhead view of the same *Grille* showing the internal layout. As well as the shell racks at the back of the fighting compartment and the charge-case boxes at the front there are more ammunition bins on the engine deck. These, like the crew seat seen, were permanent fixtures and in fact the end bin formed the rear wall of the compartment against which the doors shut. *(TM)*

RIGHT: The same *Grille*. Note that, although the division and battalion emblems were only carried on one side, the gun letter was painted on both sides. *(TM)*

LEFT: This rear view of the 2nd Panzer Division *Grille* Ausf H shows it with the doors closed. Spare track links are mounted on the back of the ammunition bin between them and both doors have mounts for equipment that has been removed, possibly for more spare track links. If anything was carried on the left door it would have covered the Division and battalion emblems, so we must assume that the original German owners deliberately removed whatever was supposed to be carried there. *(TM)*

Grille (Cricket) SdKfz 138/1 (rear-engined)

Crew	four
Combat weight, nominal	11,500kg (25,330lb)
Length	5.60m (18.37ft)
Length of hull	4.95m (16.24ft)
Width	2.15m (7.05ft)
Height	2.40m (7.87ft)
Track width	293mm (11.5in)
Max road speed	42km/h (26.1mph)
Gradient	30°
Vertical obstacle	850mm (33.5in)
Trench crossing	1.9m (6.2ft)
Fording	900mm (3.0ft)
Fuel capacity, total	280 litres (48 gallons)
Road range	185km (115 miles)
Engine	7,754cc Praga TNHPS/II six-cylinder, in-line water-cooled, petrol engine developing 150hp at 2,600rpm
Armament	one 15cm sIG 33/1 two machine pistols
HE projectile weight	38kg (83.8lb)
Barrel traverse	10°
Barrel elevation	-3° to +72°
Ammunition, 15cm	15 rounds
Ammunition, 9mm	34 rounds

Grille (Cricket) SdKfz 138/1 (mid-engined)

Crew	four
Combat weight, nominal	11,500kg (25,330lb)
Length	4.83m (15.86ft)
Length of hull	4.83m (15.86ft)
Width	2.15m (7.05ft)
Height	2.40m (7.87ft)
Track width	293mm (11.5in)
Max road speed	42km/h (26.1mph)
Gradient	30°
Vertical obstacle	850mm (33.5in)
Trench crossing	1.9m (6.2ft)
Fording	900mm (3.0ft)
Fuel capacity, total	218 litres (48 gallons)
Road range	185km (115 miles)
Engine	7,754cc Praga AC six-cylinder, in-line, water-cooled, petrol engine developing 150hp at 2,600rpm
Armament	one 15cm sIG 33/1 Two 9mm machine pistols
HE projectile weight	38kg (83.77lb)
Barrel traverse	10°
Barrel elevation	-3° to +72°
Ammunition, 15cm	15 rounds
Ammunition, 9mm	34 rounds

RIGHT: A *Grille Ausf K* at the factory with the gun at full elevation. The sprung cover for the gun opening is therefore completely closed. The supports for the canvas weather screen are interesting, with two uprights each side of the super-structure front, one each side at the rear, and a bent support each side in between. *(VF)*

BELOW RIGHT: A *Munitionspanzer 38(t)* on the Ausf K chassis. Note that it is exactly the same as the *Grille Ausf K* except for the lack of a gun. This was to allow it to be converted to a *Grille* by simply moving the gun over from a damaged *Grille*, keeping up its unit's firepower at the expense of a loss in ammunition supply carrying abilities. This factory photo-graph also shows that the tracks were painted black on new vehicles; although the paint on the track in use has already mostly worn away or been covered by dirt the spare tracks are still black. Note also that late-war tyres were no longer black but grey, due to a shortage of the carbon used to make rubber black. *(VF)*

ABOVE AND LEFT: A *Grille Ausf K* from the self-propelled artillery battalion of 1st SS Panzer Division captured in Normandy. The camouflage appears to be green patches with brown sprayed outlines over the dark yellow base coat. No tactical numbers or German crosses are carried. The blowtorch emblem, white with a red flame, is believed to be that of the battalion rather than a personal marking. *(TM)*

BELOW: The same *Grille Ausf K* allowing a rare all-round look at a single identified vehicle. The only marking on this side is the 1st SS Panzer Division's badge (key in a shield over a wreath) in white. Most of the exhaust pipe and the silencer was lost before capture. Note the typical pattern of staining on the hull side from the exhaust fumes. Modellers will note that the end of the pipe is blackened inside but does not have exhaust stains on the outside as often depicted. *(TM)*

provided on the late-production *Marder III* or *Grille* was reduced in height and given folding top plates, also it was revised to allow an all-round traverse capability for the single 2cm FlaK 38 cannon carried. The result was not a great success as the gun lacked effective range and firepower, even though 1,040 rounds were carried pre-loaded into 20-round box magazines. Cyclic rate of fire was 280rpm. This vehicle was maintained in production from late 1943 until early 1944, by which time other more effective air defence vehicles were supposed to be in the offing. A total of 141 were manufactured, the last ten examples being converted to the *Grille* configuration.

Yet More

The versatility of the original TNH-S chassis did not end with weapon carriers. A light reconnaissance model subsequently appeared, but not until after BMM had developed a similar vehicle in response to an earlier specification dating from mid-1940. The BMM submission was its TNH nA (nA – *neues Art* – new model) known to the Germans as the PzKpfw 38(t) nA, an all-round improvement over the basic TNH-S, having a slightly wider chassis, a more powerful Praga V-8 engine, a new gearbox, larger diameter road wheels, welded armour and other changes. Five prototypes were built but it did not enter production. Nevertheless by 1944 production of the vehicle then filling the tracked light reconnaissance slot, the PzKpfw II Ausf L (SdKfz 123), was coming to an end and an interim replacement was required.

Redundant PzKpfw 38(t) chassis were therefore converted for the purpose by the usual removal of the turret and fabrication of a new superstructure to carry a *2cm Hängelafette* (2cm swivelling mount), in effect a low, open-topped multi-sided turret as used on the *leichte Panzerspähwagen (2cm)* (SdKfz 222) armoured car and the SdKfz 250/9 and SdKfz 251/23 half tracks. The end result, the *Aufklärer Fahrgestell auf PzKpfw 38(t)* (SdKfz 140/1), was a perfectly serviceable light reconnaissance platform armed with a single 2cm KwK 38 cannon. It was planned that a batch of 118 would be converted by BMM using redundant light tanks but in the event only 50 such

LEFT: A *Grille Ausf K* of the 1st SS Panzer Division. The white circle on the glacis may be an official unit emblem for the division's self-propelled artillery battalion. *(TM)*

BELOW: An overhead view of a *Grille* shows the fighting compartment interior. Comparison with the Ausf H interior is interesting, with a new arrangement for the ready-round shell racks and charge cases. The radio set can be seen in the rear left corner. *(TM)*

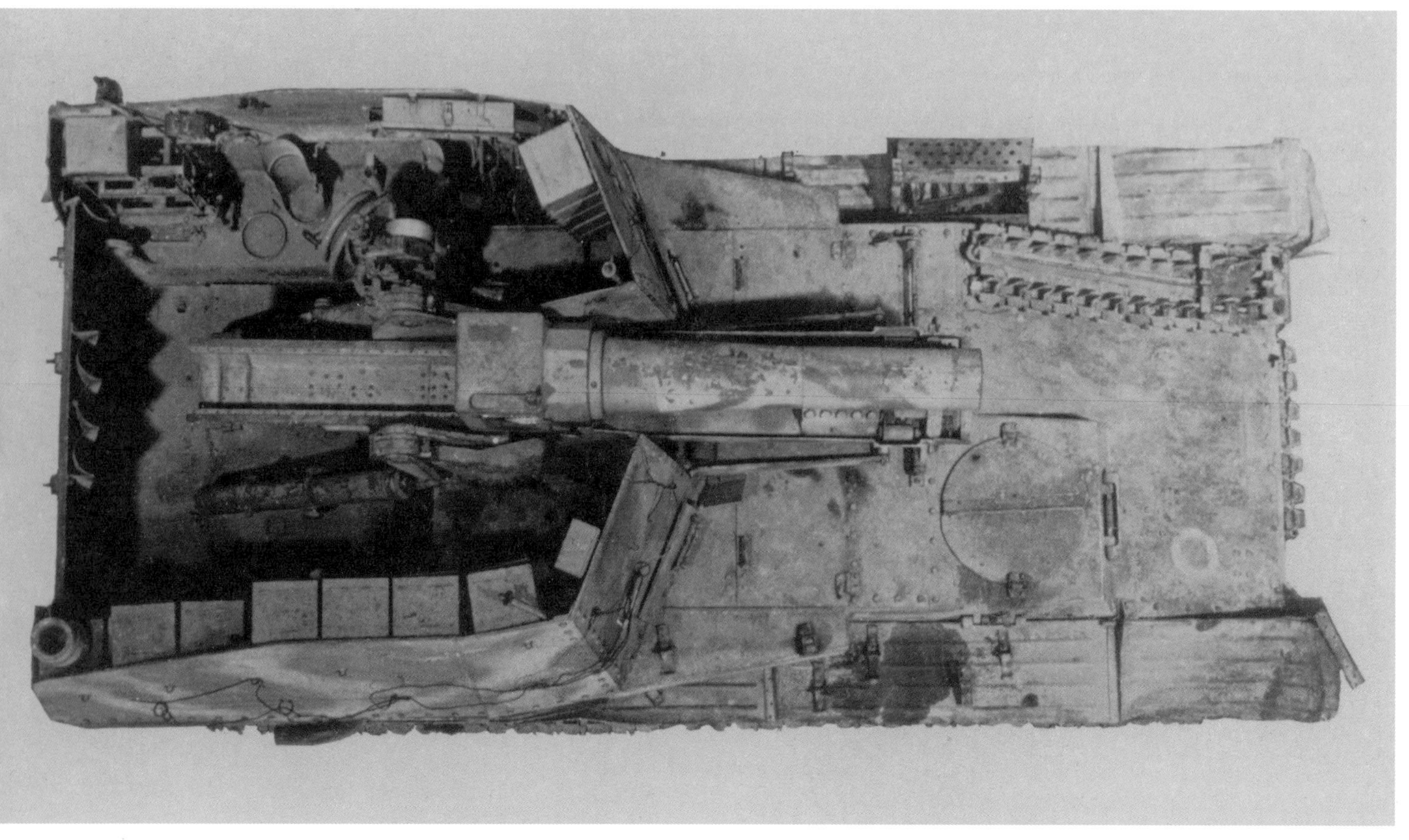

ABOVE: A *Panzerjäger 38(t) für 7.62cm PaK 36(r)* of the *Deutsches Afrika Korps* captured by the British, towing an ammunition trailer. This was usually used because of the relatively small on-board ammunition supply. *(TM)*

LEFT: The high outline of the *Panzerjäger 38(t) für 7.62cm PaK 36(r)* was a disadvantage. Against the flat desert background it was very visible. *(TM)*

LEFT: *A Flakpanzer 38(t)*, on the *Grille Ausf K* chassis. The radio antenna is mounted at an angle, but even so it needed a sprung base to be moved aside when the hinged top armour plates of the fighting compartment were lowered. *(TM)*

BELOW: A *Flakpanzer 38(t)* captured from the 12th SS Panzer Division. No other markings except German crosses are shown. The camouflage is plain dark yellow with no green or brown patches. *(TM)*

ABOVE: This view of a *Flakpanzer 38(t)* shows just how cramped were the conditions in the fighting compartment. There is barely room for the gun, so to allow the crew to move around the top plates were hinged to drop out of the way. *(TM)*

RIGHT: A 12th SS Panzer Division *Flakpanzer 38(t)*. Note the shape of the large handles fitted to the engine deck hatches. These were mounted as lifting handles and also stops to prevent the gun being fired into the driver's compartment. *(TM)*

conversions had been completed by March 1945. In addition, a close artillery fire-support vehicle similar in layout to the *Aufklärer* was proposed. Just two mock-ups mounting the stubby 7.5cm KwK 38 L/24 gun were investigated before the idea was dropped in favour of more pressing priorities.

There was one further BMM development to provide a light tracked reconnaissance vehicle but it was developed too late (late 1944) to have any affect on events. This was the *Vollkettenaufklärer 38(t) Kätzchen* (Kitten), having a lightly armoured open superstructure with provision for two machine gun mountings. It carried six to eight troops with a single entry/exit hatch provided at the rear. It remained only a prototype.

A more mundane use for redundant light tank chassis was the *Munitionschlepper auf Fahrgestell PzKpfw 38(t)*. This was a front-line ammunition carrier formed by removing the turret and erecting a canvas screen over a frame to cover the hole left by removing the turret. The crew was two and the vehicle could also tow more ammunition on trailers or sledges. Most of these vehicles retained their hull machine gun.

Another use for redundant light tanks was as the *Schulfahrerwanne PzKpfw 38(t)*. This was a driver training vehicle, nothing more than a retired light tank with the turret and armament removed. During 1944 many of these, by then ageing, training vehicles were equipped with wood-burning gas generators to conserve the dwindling stocks of more conventional fuel.

Two further new uses for the PzKpfw 38(t) chassis were investigated during 1944 but neither got past the prototype stage. One was the open-topped *Schützenpanzerwagen auf Fahrgestell PzKpfw 38(t)*. This was an armoured personnel carrier with what would normally have been the combat compartment (as on a *Marder III* on the front-engined Ausf M chassis) containing two side benches for up to eight troops. The front of the compartment was a single flat plate while two outward-opening hatches were located at the rear. Another similar but slightly shorter vehicle had sloping superstructure sides and was meant to carry a mortar up to 120mm in calibre.

ABOVE: An *Aufklärer auf Fahrgestell PzKpfw 38(t)* showing the armoured car-type turret mounted on a much-modified superstructure. The hinged screens on top of the turret were to prevent hand grenades being thrown inside. *(VF)*

ABOVE: An early *Jagdpanzer 38(t)* on trials. This vehicle shows the very early gun with a small mantlet. The photograph was taken during cross-country performance trials at the constructor's testing ground. *(VF)*

Jagdpanzer 38

The most important derivative of the PzKpfw 38(t), in both numerical and operational terms, was the little *Jagdpanzer 38*, the *Hetzer*. A fuller account of this remarkable combat vehicle is provided in Ian Allan Publishing's series *Tanks in Detail* No 9 but a summary follows

The German *Jagdpanzer* series of vehicles were developed from two sources. One was the *Panzerjäger* mobile anti-tank gun, as outlined earlier, little more than a mobile anti-tank gun platform with inadequate protection for the exposed gun and crew. The other was the well-armoured *Sturmgeschütz* assault gun. Although the *Sturmgeschütz* was operated by the artillery arm it had proved effective in the anti-armour role, so (even though it suffered from a limited-traverse gun mount) it was often deployed in Panzer formations in place of tanks. By combining the assets of both types of vehicle the *Jagdpanzer* tank destroyers emerged with powerful anti-tank guns mounted under low-profile, well-armoured carapaces.

The first *Jagdpanzer* (Hunting Tank) were based on the chassis of the PzKpfw IV tank, and proved so successful that it was planned that all PzKpfw IV production resources would be transferred to manufacturing *Jagdpanzer*. However, in 1943 *Generaloberst* Heinz Guderian, then Inspector-General of Panzer Troops, still needed new tanks to re-equip the battered Panzer divisions and sought to keep existing PzKpfw IV production lines in being to supply the much needed replacements. He had nothing against the *Jagdpanzer* concept but considered that a smaller, lighter and relatively inexpensive vehicle (*leichte Jadgpanzer*) would do everything necessary to operate as a viable tank destroyer. In March 1943 he therefore requested the development and production of such a vehicle to replace all the various improvised *Panzerjäger*. The end result was the potent *Jagdpanzer 38*, known to many as the *Hetzer*.

BMM was judged as having surplus production capacity at its disposal so it was

selected to be the prime contractor for the *leichte Jagdpanzer*. It was planned that at least 80% of the components of the PzKpfw 38(t) would be carried over to the new vehicle. The design phase for the new *leichte Jagdpanzer*, the *Gerät 555*, progressed at a commendable pace, the first vehicles being ready for troop trials during March 1944. The vehicle was based on the widened chassis used for the earlier TNH nA, the earlier light reconnaissance vehicle that was not selected for production. BMM's *leichte Jadgpanzer* featured well-sloped armour, a low silhouette and a 7.5cm PaK 39 (L/48) gun. All BMM manufacturing capacity was organised to prepare for series production of the new vehicle and Škodawerke was ordered to establish production lines at Königgrätz and Pilsen.

The *leichte Jadgpanzer* gave rise to a long list of designations. The first official title was *Sturmgeschütz neuer Art mit 7.5cm PaK 39 (L/48) auf Fahrgestell PzKpfw 38(t)* (SdKfz 138/2), but the 'soldier shorthand' name *Panzerjäger 38(t)* was more often employed. The

Jagdpanzer 38(t) Hetzer

Crew	four
Combat weight, nominal	15,750kg (34,722lb)
Length with gun	6.27m (20.73ft)
Length of hull	4.77m (15.76ft)
Width	2.53m (8.35ft)
Height	2.10m (6.9ft)
Track width	350mm (13.89in)
Max road speed	40km/h (25.1mph)
Gradient	25°
Vertical obstacle	650mm (25.79in)
Trench crossing	1.5m (5.0ft)
Fording	1.1m (3.6ft)
Fuel capacity, total	320 litres (70.4 gallons)
Road range	250km (155.3 miles)
Engine	7,754cc Praga EPA AC/2 six-cylinder in-line water-cooled petrol developing 160hp at 2,600rpm
Armament	one 7.5cm PaK 39 one 7.92mm MG 34 or MG 42
AP projectile weight	6.8kg (15lb)
Barrel traverse	5° left, 10° right
Barrel elevation	-6 to +12°
Ammunition, 7.5cm	41 rounds
Ammunition, 7.92mm	600 rounds

ABOVE: The early *Jagdpanzer 38(t),* as on the previous page, shows here the civilian number plates used during trials. Note the twin episcopes of the driver's vision port, and protruding on the roof above is the guard for the periscopic gun-sight although the sight itself is not fitted. The chassis number 231 is visible in a circle on the glacis. Modellers will note how mud has built up on the wheels and lower hull front but has not stuck to the glacis. *(TM)*

ABOVE: *Jagdpanzer 38*s carried a variety of camouflage, mostly applied at the factory. This vehicle has a late gun mantlet with a quite different shape to the early version. *(VF)*

RIGHT: A rear view shows how the discs of colour were overlapped. Even the silencer was painted, and is pristine in this factory photograph although staining at the exhaust outlet shows that the motor has been run for a short time. *(VF)*

LEFT: The gun mount. Note the bolted disc that covered the traverse pivot point inside the mount. *(TG)*

BELOW: A variation of the 'ambush' camouflage with the green and brown discs applied in patches instead of bands. Note the different idler wheel. *(VF)*

BELOW RIGHT: A *Jägdpanzer 38 Starr* built in April 1945 for a demonstration to Hitler. The *Starr* was of the fixed non-recoiling type. Note the third type of idler wheel is fitted. *(VF)*

A production-series TNH tank, for the Persian army

© 2005 Mark Franklin

LEFT: This *Jagdpanzer 38(t)* carries the later type of exhaust. Instead of a silencer mounted across the rear plate a new type is mounted on top of the engine deck. This was intended to eliminate the red glow of a hot exhaust pipe at night, but did little to reduce engine noise. *(TAn)*

LEFT: A G-13, the designation of the *Jagdpanzer 38(t)* in Swiss service, is painted in Swiss-style three-colour camouflage. *(TAn)*

PzKpfw 38(t) Ausf G

term *Jagdpanzer 38* was officially approved during November 1944, yet this handy title was often altered to *Jagdpanzer 38(t)* in many Allied references. By that period the name *Hetzer* (often translated as Baiter or Troublemaker) but perhaps it was a contraction of the word *Hetzhunde* (Hunting Dog).

Getting the combat requirements of the *Jagdpanzer 38* into the confines of such a compact vehicle formed a major technical challenge. The chassis may have been wider than that of the PzKpfw 38(t), but providing working space for the crew of four, a 7.5cm PaK 39 (L/48) gun and all the various automotive items into the limited internal volume formed an advanced armoured vehicle design exercise, especially as the armoured superstructure plates sloped inwards and further reduced the internal volume considerably. A commander, driver, gunner and loader/radio operator all had to be crammed into the interior but to do so their stations were uncomfortable and restricted to an extreme.

The hull was formed from flat, sloping, all-welded armoured steel plates. The front glacis plate was angled at 60° and was 60mm (2.36in) thick, the gun mantlet being protected by a *Topfblende* (Pot Mantlet) casting. On late production models the mantlet and *Topfblende* were reduced in size and weight with no appreciable loss in protection. Compared to the original TNH-S light tank (weight 9,850kg [21,715lb]) the combat weight of the *Jagdpanzer 38* increased to 15,750kg (34,722lb) and the increased power output (160hp) of the Praga AE petrol engine allowed a maximum road speed of 40km/h (24.5mph). Although acceleration was rated as acceptable this performance was regarded as somewhat low for the vehicle's intended combat tasks.

Getting the gun and 40 or 45 rounds of ammunition in to the combat compartment was a problem solved by a novel type of compact mounting and by offsetting the gun to the right of centre. Both the mounting and the offset severely restricted the available traverse arc to 5° left and 11° right. In addition, the compact mounting did not allow the usual installation of a defensive co-axial machine gun next to the main

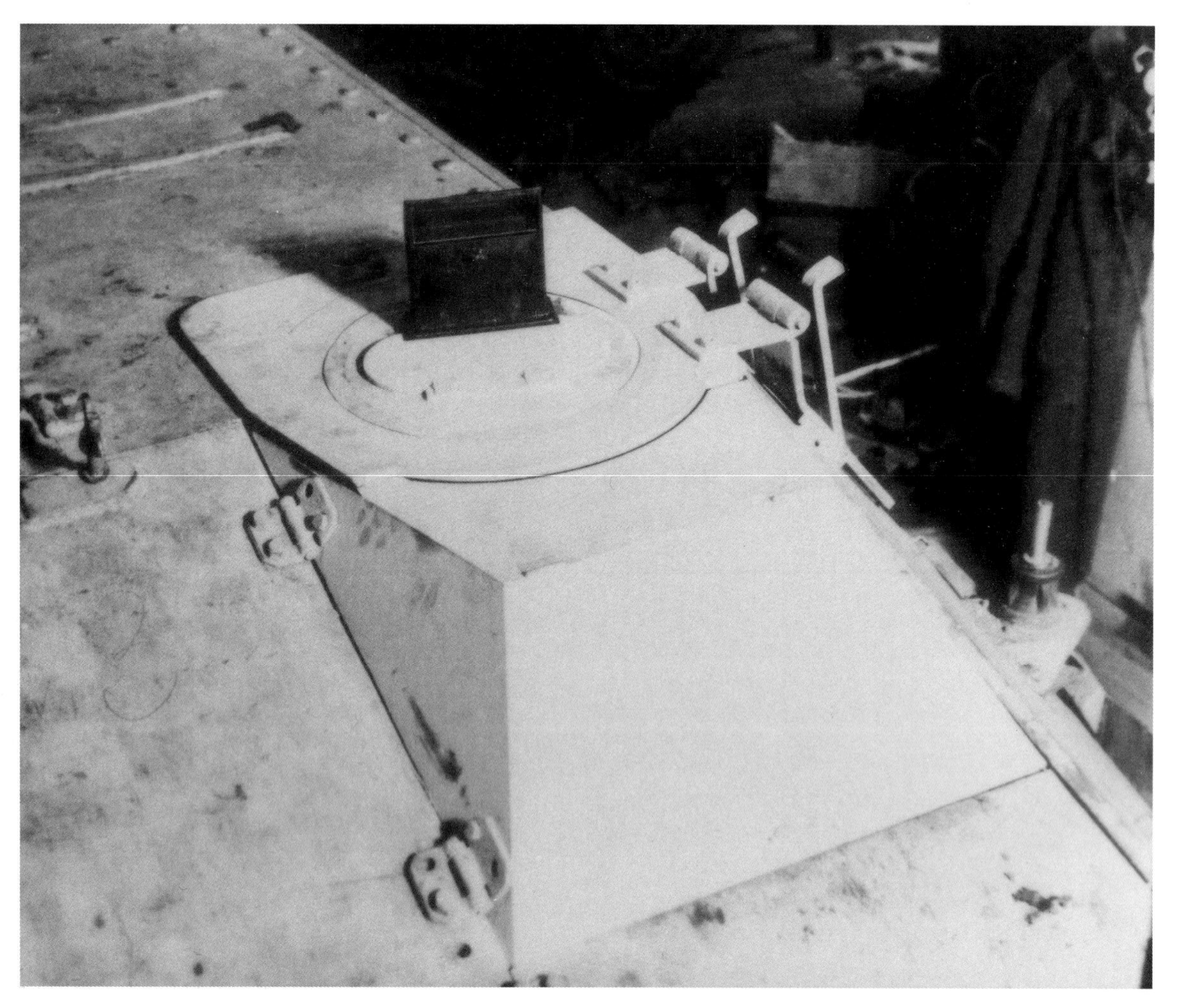

LEFT: The *Jagdpanzer 38(t) Starr* had its commander's post moved to the rear. Shown is one of the new hatch layouts tested, in this case opening to the right and with a hinged lower section opening to the left. The final design dropped the left-opening section in favour of raising the rear of the fighting compartment roof to the same extent as the hatch. The commander's periscope was mounted in a revolving base and is shown here traversed to the rear. In front of it is a flap for periscopic binoculars. *(TAn)*

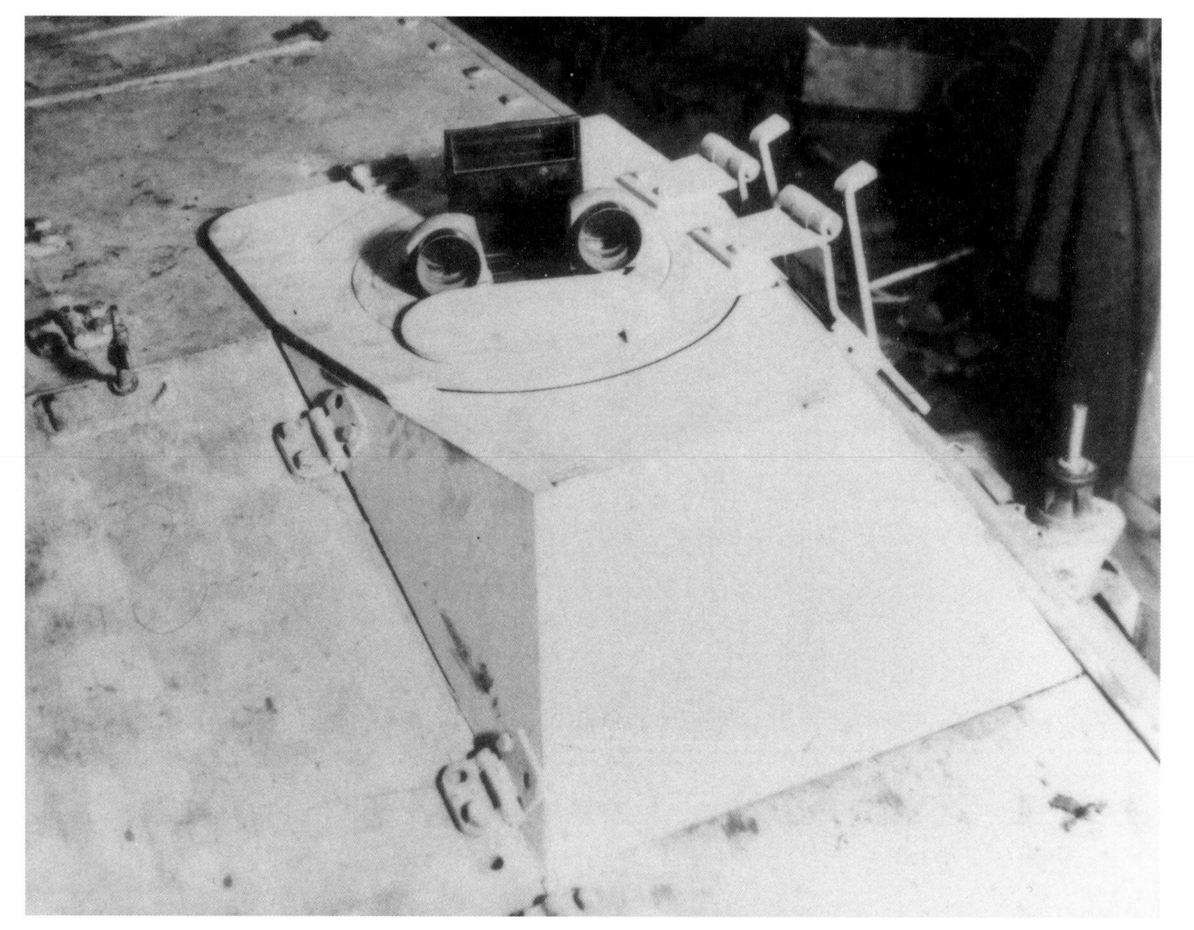

LEFT: Here the flap has been opened and the observation binoculars fitted. These were better for surveillance of the ground around the vehicle allowing a three-dimensional vision instead of the 'flat' image projected by the standard periscope. *(TAn)*

RIGHT: The *Flammpanzer 38(t)* was a *Jagdpanzer 38(t)* fitted with a flamethrower in place of the usual 75mm gun. A normal gun-shaped cover was fitted over the flamethrower tube as a disguise, but has been removed here and is on the ground in front of the vehicle. Another difference from the *Jagdpanzer 38* was the large periscope mounted on top of the hull behind the mantlet. This example was captured in the Battle of the Bulge. *(TG)*

LEFT: *A Jagdpanzer 38(t)*. Note the remote-controlled machine gun mounted on top of the fighting compartment. The gun's periscopic sight is barely visible under the barrel. *(TAn)*

BELOW: This is a perfect example of foliage camouflage. At any distance the *Jagdpanzer 38(t)* will look just like a bush, as long as the branches are renewed when the leaves change colour. *(TAn)*

RIGHT: A captured *Hetzer*. Note the crew has painted eyes on the gun mantlet. Unfortunately the unit is unknown, since any unit emblem is hidden by the foliage used as temporary camouflage. *(TAn)*

gun mounting, so instead a roof-mounted machine gun was provided.

The main gun was originally meant to be mounted in a fixed, non-recoiling *Starr* ('Inflexible', also written as *Starrer*) mounting, to simplify and speed production and also to reduce raw material and manufacturing requirements. The intention was that all recoil forces would be absorbed by the weight of the hull and chassis. The *Starr* mounting was still under development and not yet fully approved for service when the *Jagdpanzer 38* entered production so as the 7.5cm Pak 39 (L/48) was already in series production by Škodawerke it was installed from the outset. This interim measure, but it was a maintained in production until the war ended (and afterwards). Only 14 *Jagdpanzer 38 Starr* were produced for trials that were still making slow progress when the war ended. A few *Starr* models were pressed into combat in the last few days of the war.

Production of the *Jagdpanzer 38* was carried out by BMM and Škodawerke, although planned monthly targets were only rarely met. BMM was the first company to produce vehicles, with three examples ready for troop trials as early as March 1944. It was not until June 1944 that Škodawerke commenced production. By May 1945 approximately 11,000 *Jagdpanzer 38s* of all models had been ordered by the Germans, but the final total produced during the war was 2,827 plus a further batch of *Bergepanzer 38s.*

Apart from the usual *Panzerbefehlswagen 38* command vehicle variant, two other *Jagdpanzer 38* variants were produced. One was the *Flammpanzer 38* (flamethrower tank) of which 20 were produced specifically for the Ardennes offensive in late 1944. The second was a light armoured recovery vehicle, the *Bergepanzer 38* (SdKfz 136). Conversions were carried out on the BMM production lines, the final total produced ending at 181. Intended to support *Jagdpanzer 38* units in the field, the *Bergepanzer 38* had a lower, open-topped superstructure. On at least one vehicle a recovery spade was added at the rear to provide extra traction for a 5,000kg (11,023lb) recovery winch. Also carried was a collapsible 2,000kg (4,409lb) lifting jib for removing *Jagdpanzer 38* roof plates and replacing engines. The vehicle also carried specialised towing equipment and other recovery tools. In service

the *Bergepanzer 38* proved to be less than successful as the main engine proved to be underpowered. The crew remained at four and a single 7.92mm MG 34 machine gun was carried for local defence (plus the crew's personal weapons).

There was also a planned version of the *Jagdpanzer 38* mounting a suitably modified 15cm sIG 33/2 infantry support howitzer within an enlarged *Bergepanzer 38* superstructure. It was designed to meet continuing needs for a self-propelled heavy infantry gun, production of the *Grille* having ceased during February 1944.

ABOVE: A *Jagdpanzer 38* knocked out in 1944, possibly in the Battle of the Bulge. A white identification stripe has been painted on the gun mantlet and mount. *(TM)*

Production was supposed to commence during November 1944 but only a limited (but unrecorded) number were actually produced. A batch of 30 was originally planned, probably by a German manufacturer other than BMM. Some references mention this might have been Alkett of Berlin-Tegel.

The *Jagdpanzer 38* was never produced in sufficient numbers and the vehicle was not free of shortcomings, but despite these limitations the vehicle proved to be an excellent tank destroyer. It was easy to conceal, due to its low silhouette, and the main armament proved capable of knocking out all but the heaviest Allied tanks despite the aiming limits imposed by the small traverse arc. The overall automotive performance was such that the vehicle could be driven away from trouble rapidly enough when the need arose. Other unpopular features reported by *Jagdpanzer 38* crews included the cramped interior, the limited external vision when closed down, and the lack of escape hatches for those positioned to the left of the vehicle. But by 1945 the strategic situation for Germany was so desperate that such complaints simply had to be overlooked.

Panzerjäger 38(t) Hetzer (petrol) in ambush camouflage

Panzerjäger 38(t) Hetzer (diesel)

RIGHT: The low silhouette of the *Jagdpanzer 38(t)* is shown, dwarfed by the men standing on the roof. *(VF)*

LEFT: This vehicle has been thoroughly demolished, the whole roof blown off by an internal explosion, allowing a rare chance to see the right side of the gun breech. *(TAn)*

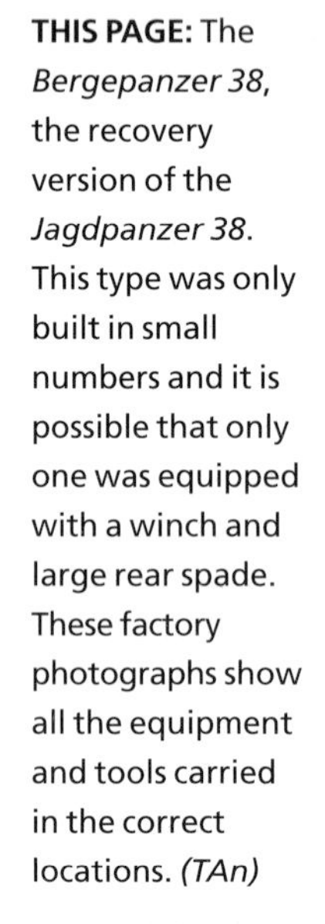

THIS PAGE: The *Bergepanzer 38*, the recovery version of the *Jagdpanzer 38*. This type was only built in small numbers and it is possible that only one was equipped with a winch and large rear spade. These factory photographs show all the equipment and tools carried in the correct locations. *(TAn)*

ABOVE: The spade-equipped *Bergepanzer 38* seen from the right-hand side. Note how the camouflage pattern has been applied over the stowed towbars but not to the wheels which are in solid single colour. *(TAn)*

RIGHT: The normal *Bergepanzer 38* had no rear spade, but did have the large heavy-duty towing bracket. The top of the right-hand side of the hull has been fitted as a stowage tray for all the small tools and tackle blocks needed in recovery tasks. *(VF)*

ABOVE: *Marder III* Ausf H being built at the factory. Although the fighting compartment is not very roomy there is clearly enough space for men to work beside the guns. *(AN)*

Production

TNH-S/PzKpfw 38(t)

Although the TNH-S light tank was intended to be issued to the Czechoslovak Army it was actually built by BMM for the Germans as the PzKpfw 38(t).

Year	1939	1940	1941	1942
January	-	10	44	59
February	-	24	50	62
March	-	34	53	28
April	-	30	49	1
May	-	30	68	21
June	21	30	57	26
July	39	38	65	-
August	18	24	64	-
September	31	35	76	-
October	30	44	53	1
November	11	27	50	-
December	-	44	49	-
Totals	150	370	678	198
Total production				**1,396**

The various model (Ausf) totals were as follows:

Ausf	A	B	C	D
	150	110	110	105
	E	F	G	S
	275	250	306	90

Variants

The total numbers of PzKpfw 38(t) variants were as follows:

SdKfz 139 (7.62cm PaK 36[r])	344
SdKfz 138 (7.5cm PaK 40)	1,217
SdKfz 138/1 (15cm sIG 33/1)	393
SdKfz 138/1 (munition carriers)	103
SdKfz 140 (2cm FlaK 38)	141
SdKfz 140/1 (light reconnaissance vehicle)	70
Total	**2,268**

PzKpfw 38(t) Ausf F

Crew	four
Combat weight, nominal	9,850kg (21,71lb)
Length with gun	4.61m (15.12ft)
Width	2.135m (8.63ft)
Height	2.17m (7ft)
Track width	293mm (11.7in)
Max road speed	42km/h (26.1mph)
Gradient	35°
Vertical obstacle	850mm (33.5in)
Trench crossing	1.9m (6.23ft)
Fording	900mm (2.95ft)
Fuel capacity, total	220-litre (48.4 UK gallons)
Road range	230km (143 miles)
Engine	7,754cc Praga EPA water-cooled, six cylinder petrol engine developing 130hp at 2,500rpm
Armament	one 3.7cm KwK 38(t) two 7.92mm MG 37(t)
AP projectile weight	1.47kg (3.24lb)
Barrel traverse	360°
Barrel elevation	-10° to +25°
Ammunition, 3.7cm	72 rounds
Ammunition, 7.92mm	2,700 rounds

RIGHT: A factory photograph of a *Jagdpanzer 38* (No. 683) being built. Note the thickness of the glacis plate armour around the aperture for the gun and mount. *(TAn)*

ABOVE: Part of the production line - the *Jagdpanzer 38*s are nearly complete, lacking only tracks and small fittings. The hatches are open but the (not yet fitted) ammunition rack is on the roof. *(TAn)*

Jagdpanzer 38

Production was split between BMM and Škodawerke:

Manufacturer	BMM	Škodawerke
1944		
March	-	3
April	20	-
May	50	-
June	100	-
July	100	10
August	150	20
September	190	30
October	133	57
November	298	89
December	223	104
1945		
January	289	145
February	273	125
March	148	153
April	70	47
Totals	**2,044**	**783**

The combined total was therefore 2,827 (although this may be an incomplete figure). To these can be added 14 *Panzerjäger Starr* variants and 181 *Bergepanzer 38* recovery vehicles, all from the BMM factory. The monthly production totals for the *Bergepanzer 38* were as follows:

1944			
May	8	June	2
July	-	August	8
September	14	October	50
November	19	December	-
1945			
January	39	February	19
March	19	April	3
		Total	**181**

ABOVE: A factory photograph shows *Jagdpanzer 38*s being built. The motors have been fitted, but the firewall to the fighting compartment is still absent. *(TAn)*

Final Total

The full total for all vehicles utilising, or based on, the TNH-S/PzKpfw 38(t) chassis was therefore 6,686, a significant proportion of the German armoured vehicle production output total between 1939 and 1945. In several references this latter total has been estimated as about 89,000 armoured vehicles of all types.

Finale

When the war ended the *Jagdpanzer 38* chassis was scheduled to form the basis for a whole array of vehicles, including its planned replacement, the *Jagdpanzer 38(d)*. For this ambitious programme the main participating contractor was no longer BMM but Alkett of Berlin-Tegel. Although only prototypes had been partially completed before the war ended, the *Jagdpanzer 38(d)* was slightly larger and heavier (combat weight 16,000kg [35,273lb]) than the basic *Jagdpanzer 38* and was intended to be powered by a 220hp Tatra TD 103 P diesel engine. The armament remained as before, although the 70-calibre 7.5cm PaK 42 (L/70) was planned as a long-term replacement. There was also mention of installing an 8.8cm PaK 43 or even some form of 12.8cm high-velocity gun.

Series production was planned to be undertaken by at least five centres at a rate of 1,250 units a month by mid-1945. The war ended before anything could materialise. An armoured personnel carrier with space for eight troops and a crew of four was just one planned variant of the *Jagdpanzer 38(d)*. Other planned variants included an armoured recovery vehicle, numerous forms of artillery and recoilless gun carrier, various turreted air defence vehicles, and a heavy mortar carrier. None of them was built.

Many other over-ambitious plans scheduled to utilise the basic PzKpfw 38(t) chassis in much-modified forms were terminated by the end of war, usually involving widened hulls and/or an extra set of road wheels. These plans covered all manner of types, from *leichte* (light) and *mittlere* (medium) *Waffenträger* (weapon carriers) intended to carry artillery pieces or heavy anti-tank guns, to artillery direct fire support weapon carriers mounting an array of weapons. Once again, BMM had little design input into the *Waffenträger* project as the design responsibility was transferred to Ardelt, Krupp or Rheinmetall-Borsig, depending on the weapon carried. No doubt BMM would have retained some part in the manufacture of the chassis, drive train and running gear.

While many of these advanced concepts, such as the *Waffenträger*, had no direct counterparts in the Allied wartime combat vehicle fleets, many of the ideas did materialise post-war on other chassis. Yet in retrospect it seems unlikely that the *Waffenträger* concept could have lasted long for it was primarily intended to carry an artillery piece to its firing position and then unload it for ground firing. This approach obviously had few attractions for post-war gunners. Their long-term solution was the more mobile, versatile and easier to handle self-propelled artillery piece.

All of these unpredicted combat vehicle roles were a long way from the original ČKD TNH-S light tank.

BELOW: The prototype of the postwar MP-1 flamethrower tank built for the Czech Army, the final vehicle on a PzKpfw 38(t) chassis. A number of *Jagdpanzer 38*s were in store and a flamethrower tank was needed, so a conversion was designed with the original gun opening plated over and a round turret added to the roof for the flamethrower. *(VF)*

RIGHT: A set of photographs showing all aspects of the MP-1. Ancestry from the *Jagdpanzer 38* is clear, but the turret changes the appearance considerably. A large armoured housing was added to the side to hold the cylinders of compressed air used to project the flame. The flame fuel was carried inside the tank. A Soviet *Degtyarev* machine gun was to be fitted in the turret beside the flamethrower. Note the location for the flexible mount. The prototype was modified several times but by 1955 when the final design was finished the Czech Army had lost interest so the remainder of the 75 planned conversions were never built. *(TAn)*

ABOVE AND LEFT: The *leichter Waffenträger* built with PzKpfw 38(t) components in 1944. The intention was to have a chassis capable of carrying the 8.8cm anti-tank gun, to be dismountable for emplacement on the ground. Although the design was accepted for production the end of the war meant that only a very few were built and as far as is known never used in combat service. *(VF)*

LEFT: This vehicle is clearly based on the *Jagdpanzer 38* chassis, but when and by whom the crane was added is unknown. It is just one of the postwar conversions made to all kinds of vehicles. *(TAn)*